DON WILLIAMS
CELEBRATE
YOUR
FREEDOM

AN INDUCTIVE BIBLE STUDY
ON GALATIANS

Word Books, Publisher

Waco, Texas

To
Randy and Ann Smith
who fulfill the law of Christ
(Galatians 6:2)

Contents

Part One

An Overview of Galatians

Galatians is a tract for our times. With punch and power it devastates the relativism and performance characteristic of our culture. This letter finds the Apostle Paul at his white-heat best. He is on the offensive–defensive with his call, message, and lifestyle under attack. "Paul is no apostle," his opponents say. "His gospel is a perversion—too simple. He is promoting moral anarchy." Hearing these charges, the Apostle, like a cornered animal, bares his fangs. He lashes out with history, theology, ethics, and exhortation, all focused under intense pressure. The results are a few short pages which present and defend Christian freedom trenchantly.

Let us now enter Paul's world of conflict by looking closely at the letter.

In order to get a feel for the Book of Galatians, let us go through the above process step-by-step.

1.

Paul's letters are not written in a vacuum. When we understand his goals in writing, we begin to uncover his strategy and tactics in reaching those goals. Our task is to see Galatians as a whole and determine the situations of both Paul and his churches which produced the letter. Using the text of the Revised Standard Version, then, let us *read Galatians through and make up paragraph titles for our overview,* inserting them in the spaces provided before each paragraph.

1:1–2 Title _____
Paul an apostle—not from men nor through man, but through Jesus Christ and God the Father, who raised him from the dead—[2] and all the brethren who are with me,
To the churches of Galatia:

1:3–5 Title _____
[3] Grace to you and peace from God the Father and our Lord Jesus Christ, [4] who gave himself for our sins to deliver us from the present evil age, according to the will of our God and Father; [5] to whom be the glory for ever and ever. Amen.

1:6–9 Title _____
[6] I am astonished that you are so quickly deserting him who called you in the grace of Christ and turning to a different gospel—[7] not that there is another gospel, but there are some who trouble you and want to pervert the gospel of Christ. [8] But even if we, or an angel from heaven, should preach to you a gospel contrary to that which we preached to you, let him be accursed. [9] As we have said before, so now I say again, If any one is preaching to you a gospel contrary to that which you received, let him be accursed.

11

1:10 Title _____

¹⁰ Am I now seeking the favor of men, or of God? Or am I trying to please men? If I were still pleasing men, I should not be a servant of Christ.

1:11–17 Title _____

¹¹ For I would have you know, brethren, that the gospel which was preached by me is not man's gospel. ¹² For I did not receive it from man, nor was I taught it, but it came through a revelation of Jesus Christ. ¹³ For you have heard of my former life in Judaism, how I persecuted the church of God violently and tried to destroy it; ¹⁴ and I advanced in Judaism beyond many of my own age among my people, so extremely zealous was I for the traditions of my fathers. ¹⁵ But when he who had set me apart before I was born, and had called me through his grace, ¹⁶ was pleased to reveal his Son to me, in order that I might preach him among the Gentiles, I did not confer with flesh and blood, ¹⁷ nor did I go up to Jerusalem to those who were apostles before me, but I went away into Arabia; and again I returned to Damascus.

1:18–24 Title _____

¹⁸ Then after three years I went up to Jerusalem to visit Cephas, and remained with him fifteen days. ¹⁹ But I saw none of the other apostles except James the Lord's brother. ²⁰ (In what I am writing to you, before God, I do not lie!) ²¹ Then I went into the regions of Syria and Cilicia. ²² And I was still not known by sight to the churches of Christ in Judea; ²³ they only heard it said, "He who once persecuted us is now preaching the faith he once tried to destroy." ²⁴ And they glorified God because of me.

2:1–10 Title _____

Then after fourteen years I went up again to Jerusalem with Barnabas, taking Titus along with me. ² I went up by revelation; and I laid before them (but privately before those who were of repute) the gospel which I preach among the Gentiles, lest somehow I should be running or had run in vain. ³ But even Titus, who was with me, was not compelled to be circumcised, though he was a Greek. ⁴ But because of false brethren secretly brought in, who slipped in to spy out our freedom which we have in Christ Jesus, that they might bring us into bondage—⁵ to them we did not yield submission even for a moment, that the truth of the gospel might be preserved for you. ⁶ And from those who were reputed to be something (what they were makes no difference to me; God shows no partiality)—those, I say, who were of repute added nothing to me; ⁷ but on the contrary, when they saw that I had been entrusted with the gospel to the uncircumcised, just as Peter had been entrusted with the gospel to the circumcised ⁸ (for he who worked through Peter for the mission to the circumcised worked through me also for the Gentiles), ⁹ and when they perceived the grace that was given to me, James and Cephas and John, who were reputed to be pillars, gave to me and Barnabas the right hand of fellowship, that we should go to the Gentiles

and they to the circumcised; ¹⁰ only they would have us remember the
poor, which very thing I was eager to do.

2:11–21 Title   ————————————————————

¹¹ But when Cephas came to Antioch I opposed him to his face, because he
stood condemned. ¹² For before certain men came from James, he ate with
the Gentiles; but when they came he drew back and separated himself, fearing the circumcision party. ¹³ And with him the rest of the Jews acted insincerely, so that even Barnabas was carried away by their insincerity. ¹⁴ But
when I saw that they were not straightforward about the truth of the gospel,
I said to Cephas before them all, "If you, though a Jew, live like a Gentile
and not like a Jew, how can you compel the Gentiles to live like Jews?"
¹⁵ We ourselves, who are Jews by birth and not Gentile sinners, ¹⁶ yet who
know that a man is not justified by works of the law but through faith
in Jesus Christ, even we have believed in Christ Jesus, in order to be justified
by faith in Christ, and not by works of the law, because by works of the
law shall no one be justified. ¹⁷ But if, in our endeavor to be justified in
Christ, we ourselves were found to be sinners, is Christ then an agent of
sin? Certainly not! ¹⁸ But if I build up again those things which I tore down,
then I prove myself a transgressor. ¹⁹ For I through the law died to the
law, that I might live to God. ²⁰ I have been crucified with Christ; it is no
longer I who live, but Christ who lives in me; and the life I now live in the
flesh I live by faith in the Son of God, who loved me and gave himself for
me. ²¹ I do not nullify the grace of God; for if justification were through the
law, then Christ died to no purpose.

3:1–5 Title   ————————————————————

O foolish Galatians! Who has bewitched you, before whose eyes Jesus Christ
was publicly portrayed as crucified? ² Let me ask you only this: Did you
receive the Spirit by works of the law, or by hearing with faith? ³ Are you so
foolish? Having begun with the Spirit, are you now ending with the flesh?
⁴ Did you experience so many things in vain?—if it really is in vain. ⁵ Does
he who supplies the Spirit to you and works miracles among you do so by
works of the law, or by hearing with faith?

3:6–9 Title   ————————————————————

⁶ Thus Abraham "believed God, and it was reckoned to him as righteous-
ness." ⁷ So you see that it is men of faith who are the sons of Abraham. ⁸ And
the scripture, foreseeing that God would justify the Gentiles by faith, preached
the gospel beforehand to Abraham, saying, "In you shall all the nations be
blessed." ⁹ So then, those who are men of faith are blessed with Abraham
who had faith.

3:10–14 Title   ————————————————————

¹⁰ For all who rely on works of the law are under a curse; for it is written,
"Cursed be every one who does not abide by all things written in the book

of the law, and do them." [11] Now it is evident that no man is justified before God by the law; for "He who through faith is righteous shall live"; [12] but the law does not rest on faith, for "He who does them shall live by them." [13] Christ redeemed us from the curse of the law, having become a curse for us—for it is written, "Cursed be every one who hangs on a tree"—[14] that in Christ Jesus the blessing of Abraham might come upon the Gentiles, that we might receive the promise of the Spirit through faith.

3:15–18 Title _____

[15] To give a human example, brethren: no one annuls even a man's will, or adds to it, once it has been ratified. [16] Now the promises were made to Abraham and to his offspring. It does not say, "And to offsprings," referring to many; but, referring to one, "And to your offspring," which is Christ. [17] This is what I mean: the law, which came four hundred and thirty years afterward, does not annul a covenant previously ratified by God, so as to make the promise void. [18] For if the inheritance is by the law, it is no longer by promise; but God gave it to Abraham by a promise.

3:19–20 Title _____

[19] Why then the law? It was added because of transgressions, till the offspring should come to whom the promise had been made; and it was ordained by angels through an intermediary. [20] Now an intermediary implies more than one; but God is one.

3:21–22 Title _____

[21] Is the law then against the promises of God? Certainly not; for if a law had been given which could make alive, then righteousness would indeed be by the law. [22] But the scripture consigned all things to sin, that what was promised to faith in Jesus Christ might be given to those who believe.

3:23–29 Title _____

[23] Now before faith came, we were confined under the law, kept under restraint until faith should be revealed. [24] So that the law was our custodian until Christ came, that we might be justified by faith. [25] But now that faith has come, we are no longer under a custodian; [26] for in Christ Jesus you are all sons of God, through faith. [27] For as many of you as were baptized into Christ have put on Christ. [28] There is neither Jew nor Greek, there is neither slave nor free, there is neither male nor female; for you are all one in Christ Jesus. [29] And if you are Christ's, then you are Abraham's offspring, heirs according to promise.

4:1–7 Title _____

I mean that the heir, as long as he is a child, is no better than a slave, though he is the owner of all the estate; [2] but he is under guardians and trustees until the date set by the father. [3] So with us; when we were children, we were slaves to the elemental spirits of the universe. [4] But when the time had fully come, God sent forth his Son, born of woman, born under the law, [5] to redeem those who were under the law, so that we might receive adoption as sons. [6] And because you are sons, God has sent the Spirit of his Son into our hearts, crying, "Abba! Father!" [7] So through God you are no longer a slave but a son, and if a son then an heir.

4:8–11 Title ───────────────────────

[8] Formerly, when you did not know God, you were in bondage to beings that by nature are no gods; [9] but now that you have come to know God, or rather to be known by God, how can you turn back again to the weak and beggarly elemental spirits, whose slaves you want to be once more? [10] You observe days, and months, and seasons, and years! [11] I am afraid I have labored over you in vain.

4:12–20 Title ───────────────────────

[12] Brethren, I beseech you, become as I am, for I also have become as you are. You did me no wrong; [13] you know it was because of a bodily ailment that I preached the gospel to you at first; [14] and though my condition was a trial to you, you did not scorn or despise me, but received me as an angel of God, as Christ Jesus. [15] What has become of the satisfaction you felt? For I bear witness that, if possible, you would have plucked out your eyes and given them to me. [16] Have I then become your enemy by telling you the truth? [17] They make much of you, but for no good purpose; they want to shut you out, that you may make much of them. [18] For a good purpose it is always good to be made much of, and not only when I am present with you. [19] My little children, with whom I am again in travail until Christ be formed in you! [20] I could wish to be present with you now and to change my tone, for I am perplexed about you.

4:21–31 Title ───────────────────────

[21] Tell me, you who desire to be under law, do you not hear the law? [22] For it is written that Abraham had two sons, one by a slave and one by a free woman. [23] But the son of the slave was born according to the flesh, the son of the free woman through promise. [24] Now this is an allegory: these women are two covenants. One is from Mount Sinai, bearing children for slavery; she is Hagar. [25] Now Hagar is Mount Sinai in Arabia; she corresponds to the present Jerusalem, for she is in slavery with her children. [26] But the Jerusalem above is free, and she is our mother. [27] For it is written,

"Rejoice, O barren one that dost not bear;

break forth and shout, thou who are not in travail;

for the desolate hath more children than she who hath a husband."

[28] Now we, brethren, like Isaac, are children of promise. [29] But as at that time he who was born according to the flesh persecuted him who was born according to the Spirit, so it is now. [30] But what does the scripture say? "Cast out the slave and her son; for the son of the slave shall not inherit

with the son of the free woman." [31] So, brethren, we are not children of the slave but of the free woman.

5:1 Title ————————————————

For freedom Christ has set us free; stand fast therefore, and do not submit again to a yoke of slavery.

5:2–12 Title ————————————————

[2] Now I, Paul, say to you that if you receive circumcision, Christ will be of no advantage to you. [3] I testify again to every man who receives circumcision that he is bound to keep the whole law. [4] You are severed from Christ, you who would be justified by the law; you have fallen away from grace. [5] For through the Spirit, by faith, we wait for the hope of righteousness. [6] For in Christ Jesus neither circumcision nor uncircumcision is of any avail, but faith working through love. [7] You were running well; who hindered you from obeying the truth? [8] This persuasion is not from him who called you. [9] A little leaven leavens the whole lump. [10] I have confidence in the Lord that you will take no other view than mine; and he who is troubling you will bear his judgment, whoever he is. [11] But if I, brethren, still preach circumcision, why am I still persecuted? In that case the stumbling block of the cross has been removed. [12] I wish those who unsettle you would mutilate themselves.

5:13–15 Title ————————————————

[13] For you were called to freedom, brethren; only do not use your freedom as an opportunity for the flesh, but through love be servants of one another. [14] For the whole law is fulfilled in one word, "You shall love your neighbor as yourself." [15] But if you bite and devour one another take heed that you are not consumed by one another.

5:16–24 Title ————————————————

[16] But I say, walk by the Spirit, and do not gratify the desires of the flesh. [17] For the desires of the flesh are against the Spirit, and the desires of the Spirit are against the flesh; for these are opposed to each other, to prevent you from doing what you would. [18] But if you are led by the Spirit you are not under the law. [19] Now the works of the flesh are plain: immorality, impurity, licentiousness, [20] idolatry, sorcery, enmity, strife, jealousy, anger, selfishness, dissension, party spirit, [21] envy, drunkenness, carousing, and the like. I warn you, as I warned you before, that those who do such things shall not inherit the kingdom of God. [22] But the fruit of the Spirit is love, joy, peace, patience, kindness, goodness, faithfulness, [23] gentleness, self-control; against such there is no law. [24] And those who belong to Christ Jesus have crucified the flesh with its passions and desires.

5:25–26 Title ————————————————

[25] If we live by the Spirit, let us also walk by the Spirit. [26] Let us have no self-conceit, no provoking of one another, no envy of one another.

6:1–5 Title _____

Brethren, if a man is overtaken in any trespass, you who are spiritual should restore him in a spirit of gentleness. Look to yourself, lest you too be tempted. ² Bear one another's burdens, and so fulfil the law of Christ. ³ For if any one thinks he is something, when he is nothing, he deceives himself. ⁴ But let each one test his own work, and then his reason to boast will be in himself alone and not in his neighbor. ⁵ For each man will have to bear his own load.

6:6 Title _____

⁶ Let him who is taught the word share all good things with him who teaches.

6:7–10 Title _____

⁷ Do not be deceived; God is not mocked, for whatever a man sows, that he will also reap. ⁸ For he who sows to his own flesh will from the flesh reap corruption; but he who sows to the Spirit will from the Spirit reap eternal life. ⁹ And let us not grow weary in well-doing, for in due season we shall reap, if we do not lose heart. ¹⁰ So then, as we have opportunity, let us do good to all men, and especially to those who are of the household of faith.

6:11–16 Title _____

¹¹ See with what large letters I am writing to you with my own hand. ¹² It is those who want to make a good showing in the flesh that would compel you to be circumcised, and only in order that they may not be persecuted for the cross of Christ. ¹³ For even those who receive circumcision do not themselves keep the law, but they desire to have you circumcised that they may glory in your flesh. ¹⁴ But far be it from me to glory except in the cross of our Lord Jesus Christ, by which the world has been crucified to me, and I to the world. ¹⁵ For neither circumcision counts for anything, nor uncircumcision, but a new creation. ¹⁶ Peace and mercy be upon all who walk by this rule, upon the Israel of God.

6:17 Title _____

¹⁷ Henceforth let no man trouble me; for I bear on my body the marks of Jesus.

6:18 Title _____

¹⁸ The grace of our Lord Jesus Christ be with your spirit, brethren. Amen.

Now Compare Your Work with Mine

1:1–2——Salutation: Paul to the Galatians; defense of his apostleship.

1:3–5——Blessing: a statement of Paul's gospel.

1:6–9——The Galatians are deserting the gospel through "troublers" perverting them.

1:10——Paul seeks not to please men but God.

1:11–17——Thesis: Paul's gospel came by revelation—the recall of his life in Judaism and in Christ.

1:18–24——Paul's independence from Jerusalem: his first visit.

2:1–10——The truth of the gospel defended at Jerusalem: his second visit.

2:11–21——The truth of the gospel defended at Antioch: Paul vs. Peter.

3:1–5——The experience of the Galatians confirms the truth of Paul's gospel "by faith."

3:6–9——The gospel came as a promise to Abraham.

3:10–14——Christ frees us from the curse of the law and fulfills Abraham's promise of blessing.

3:15–18——The law cannot annul the promise: it came later.

3:19–20——The law was added because of transgressions.

3:21–22——The law reveals sin.

3:23–29——The law remained until faith came; we are all now one in Christ.

4:1–7——We were guarded by law until the time fully came: now we are sons and heirs.

4:8–11——How can you turn back to the old bondage?

4:12–20——Paul's relations with the Galatians: warmth before, perplexity now.

4:21–31——Allegory from Abraham: slave and free.

5:1——Stand fast in freedom.

5:2–12——The Christian life: not circumcision, but faith working through love.

5:13–15——Freedom to love is freedom to serve.

5:16–24——Freedom to walk by the Spirit bearing his fruit, not to gratify the flesh doing its works.

5:25–26——Walk by the Spirit without selfishness.

6:1–5——Caring for the brethren.

6:6——Sharing in teaching.

6:7–10——The law of sowing and reaping bears its fruit.

6:11–16——Paul's autograph—not circumcision but the cross.

6:17——Paul's marks are from Jesus.

6:18——Benediction.

2.

With this overview before us, we are now ready to *re-create the historical situation* out of which Galatians has come. Our one objective source is the letter itself.

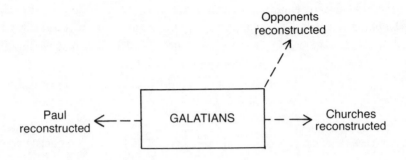

Much of Galatians describes Paul's past experiences which make up his present attitude; to understand Galatians we must understand Paul. As we study, he begins to emerge as a person:

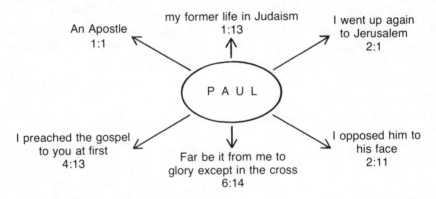

Also we must understand his churches. Much of Paul's attitude is determined by what is going on there.

The churches of Galatia begin to emerge as real churches:

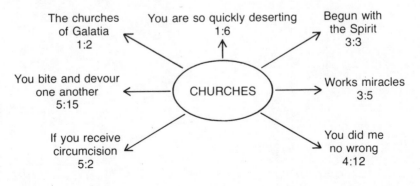

Now we begin to see the strengths, weaknesses, and needs of these new Christians. Their experiences too have formed this letter—especially their experiences with the opponents who want to undo Paul's work.

The opponents now begin to come into focus:

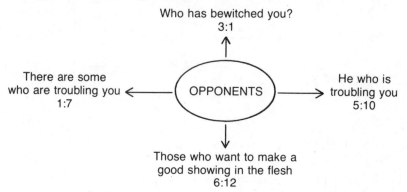

Now we are ready to *collect all the evidence for our historical reconstruction of Paul, the Galatians, and their opponents.* Using the columns below fill in the blanks with a summary of the material in each verse. Note that in 1:10, 11, 17 and 2:3 and 2:6 we ask for an inference from Paul's argument as to the charges brought against him by his opponents. Think about what he is responding to. Feel free to add anything else you discover in your study.

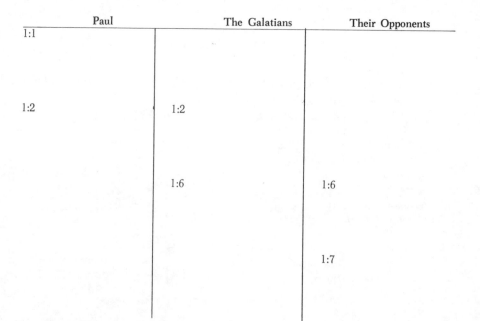

Paul	The Galatians	Their Opponents
1:1		
1:2	1:2	
	1:6	1:6
		1:7

Paul	The Galatians	Their Opponents
1:8		1:8
	1:9	1:9
1:10		1:10 (Inference)
1:11		1:11 (Inference)
1:12		
1:13		
1:14		
1:15		
1:16		

Paul	The Galatians	Their Opponents
1:17		1:17 (Inference)
1:18		
1:19		
1:21		
1:22		
1:23		
1:24		
2:1		
2:2		

Paul	The Galatians	Their Opponents
2:3		2:3 (Inference)
2:4–5		
2:6		2:6 (Inference)
2:7		
2:8		
2:9		
2:10		
2:11		
2:12–13		

	Paul	The Galatians	Their Opponents
2:14			
2:15–16			
		3:1	
		3:2	
		3:3	
		3:4	
		3:5	
		3:27–28	
		4:3	

Paul	The Galatians	Their Opponents
	4:8	
	4:9	
	4:10	
4:11		
4:12	4:12	
4:13		
4:14	4:14	
	4:15	
4:16		

Paul	The Galatians	Their Opponents
	4:17	4:17
4:18		
4:19		
4:20		
	4:21	
	5:1	
	5:2–3	
	5:7	5:7–8
		5:10

Paul	The Galatians	Their Opponents
5:11		
5:12		5:12
	5:15	
6:11		
	6:12	6:12
		6:13
6:17		

If you have any problems, compare your work with mine below. Do you agree or disagree? Why?

Paul	The Galatians	Their Opponents
1:1—Apostle—not human but divine authority by God and the risen Christ		
1:2—Brethren with Paul	1:2—Churches (plural)	
	1:6—Quickly deserting God and turning to another gospel	1:6—Another gospel

Paul	The Galatians	Their Opponents
		1:7—Troublers who pervert the gospel
1:8—We preached the gospel to you		1:8—A contrary gospel
	1:9—Hearing a contrary gospel—they received the true gospel	1:9—A gospel contrary
1:10—Not a manpleaser; serves Christ		1:10—Inference: charge Paul is a manpleaser
1:11—Preaches the gospel, not man's creation		1:11—Inference: charge Paul preaches man's gospel
1:12—Gospel not received or taught, divine revelation		
1:13—Former life in Judaism, persecuted the church		
1:14—Advanced in Judaism, zealous for traditions		
1:15—Set apart before birth, called by grace		
1:16—The Son revealed in Paul—call to preach—no human conference		
1:17—No Jerusalem visit to the apostles—Arabia and Damascus		1:17—Inference: Paul dependent on Jerusalem
1:18—Jerusalem after 3 years to visit Cephas 15 days		
1:19—Also only James the Lord's brother		
1:20—Writes the truth		
1:21—Syria and Cilicia visits		
1:22—Unknown by sight in the Judean churches		
1:23—"Once persecuted," "now preaching"		
1:24—God glorified because of Paul		
2:1—Jerusalem after 14 years with Barnabas and Titus		
2:2—Went by revelation. Explained his gospel privately to those of repute		

Paul	The Galatians	Their Opponents
2:3—Titus, though Greek, not compelled to be circumcised		2:3—Inference: Titus was circumcised
2:4–5—False brethren spying out freedom—Paul doesn't yield to preserve the gospel		
2:6—Those of repute added nothing		2:6—Inference: much added to his gospel
2:7—They saw—Paul to Gentiles, Peter to Jews		
2:8—God worked through Peter and Paul		
2:9—James, Cephas and John—give fellowship to Paul and Barnabas—Division of labor to Jews and Gentiles		
2:10—Condition: remember the poor—Paul eager to do		
2:11—Cephas to Antioch, opposed by Paul		
2:12–13—Cephas and Barnabas ate with Gentiles, but withdrew before certain men from James, the circumcision party		
2:14—Paul rebukes Cephas for hypocrisy		
2:15–16—Even "we Jews," not "Gentile sinners," know we are justified by faith		
	3:1—Foolish and bewitched. Christ crucified preached publicly to them	
	3:2—Received the Spirit by hearing with faith	
	3:3—Foolish—begun as with the Spirit and now ending with the flesh	
	3:4—They all experienced many things	
	3:5—Spirit and miracles manifested by faith	
	3:27–28—All baptized into Christ, therefore, all one in Christ—Jew and Greek, slave and free, male and female	

Paul	The Galatians	Their Opponents
	4:3—Children: slaves to the elemental spirits of the universe	
	4:8—Formerly, not know God, in bondage to "no gods"	
	4:9—Turning back to the weak and beggarly elemental spirits—slaves again	
	4:10—Observing the days, months, seasons, years	
4:11—Fears labor in vain		
4:12—Became as the Galatians were	4:12—Did Paul no wrong	
4:13—Preached because of a bodily ailment		
4:14—Condition a trial to them	4:14—Not reject Paul—received as Christ himself	
	4:15—They felt satisfaction —would have given Paul their eyes	
4:16—Telling them the truth		
	4:17—Being made much of by the opponents	4:17—Make much of the Galatians—no good purpose —want to shut them out
4:18—Made much of by the Galatians when with them		
4:19—In travail until Christ formed in them		
4:20—Desires to be present —perplexed		
	4:21—Desire to be under law	
	5:1—Danger of submitting again to a yoke of bondage	
	5:2–3—Danger of receiving circumcision	
	5:7—Were running well	5:7–8—Hinder the Galatians from obeying the truth—a false persuasion
		5:10—Someone is troubling them
5:11—Paul does not preach circumcision—therefore persecuted		

Paul	The Galatians	Their Opponents
5:12—Desires the opponents to mutilate themselves		5:12—Unsettlers
	5:15—Danger of biting and devouring each other	
6:11—Writes with large letters in own hand		
	6:12—Being compelled to be circumcised	6:12—Desire to make a good showing in the flesh and not be persecuted for the cross
		6:13—Not keep the law—want to glory in the Galatians' flesh.
6:17—Bears on his body the marks of Jesus		

3.

With the raw materials before us for reconstructing the historical setting of the letter, *summarize Paul's situation, the Galatians' situation and the opponents.*

Paul

1. His former life in Judaism:

2. His conversion:

3. His sense of calling and mission:

4. His message:

5. His relationship to the Jerusalem Church and other apostles:

6. His relationship to the Galatians:

The Galatians

1. Their pre-Christian experience:

2. Their conversion to Christ:

3. Their present experience and stability:

The Opponents

1. The sources of the opposition:

2. The claims against Paul:

3. The nature of the opposition:

(Now compare your summaries with mine)

Paul

1. His former life in Judaism:

Paul was a Jew by birth (2:15). As such he was bound to keep the whole law (5:3). While zealous for the Jewish traditions, he advanced beyond many of his own peer group (1:14). Not only did he preach circumcision (5:11), but he also violently persecuted the church and tried to destroy it (1:13, 23).

2. His conversion:

Paul became a Christian through God's plan established before his birth (1:15). The grace of God which called Paul became effective when the Son was revealed "to" or "in" him (1:16). This relieved him from keeping the Jewish law as he placed his faith in Jesus Christ (2:16).

3. His sense of calling and mission:

Paul is now an apostle of Jesus Christ by direct divine call (1:1). Thus he is a servant of Christ. Since his call at conversion was to preach Christ among the Gentiles (1:16 and 2:2), he bears the gospel to the uncircumcised (2:7), and God works through him (2:8).

4. His message:

Paul's gospel, as his calling, came by direct revelation (1:12). In that sense it is not man's gospel (1:11). It centers in a person: Jesus Christ

(1:16), whom Paul publicly portrays as crucified (3:1). While as old as God's promise to Abraham (3:8), it has now been realized in Christ (3:14), who has taken the curse of the law from us in His death and given us the spirit by faith (3:13–14).

5. His relationship to the Jerusalem church and other apostles:

Paul is independent of any human authority for his gospel or calling (1:12 and 1:16). Only after three years did he confer with Cephas and James in Jerusalem for fifteen days (1:18–19). After fourteen years he went up to Jerusalem with Barnabas and Titus (2:1) to defend the truth of the gospel (2:5). Paul privately presented his message and ministry to those of repute (2:2) and they added nothing to it (2:6). The right hand of fellowship and an exhortation to remember the poor was all that was asked of him (2:9–10). Later in Antioch Paul opposed Cephas because of his hypocrisy in not eating with the Gentiles (2:11–12). Thus in all his relationships with the apostles, Paul experiences independence, equality and their confirmation of his calling.

6. His relationship to the Galatians:

Paul preached the gospel to the Galatians (1:8, 1:11 and 4:13) because of a physical illness which sent him into their area (4:13). He identified with them (4:12), although his condition was a trial (4:14) as he labored over them (4:11). Now in travail again (4:19), Paul wishes to be present and resolve his perplexity, since they are his little children (4:19).

The Galatians

1. Their pre-Christian experience:

Formerly, as pagans, the Galatians did not know God and were in bondage to idols (4:8). Thus they were slaves to the weak and beggarly elemental spirits of the universe (4:9).

2. Their conversion to Christ:

The Galatians received Paul as an angel, as Christ himself (4:14). They felt such satisfaction, they would have plucked out their eyes and given them to him (4:15). As the crucified Christ was presented before them (3:1), they received the Spirit by believing in the gospel (3:2).

Beginning in the Spirit they experienced miracles (3:5), were baptized into Christ (3:27) and were running well (5:7).

3. Their present experience and stability:

The Galatians are now quickly deserting the God who called them (1:16). Being foolish and bewitched (3:1), they are ending in the flesh (3:3), turning back to the weak and beggarly elemental spirits (4:9) and becoming enslaved to them by observing days, months, seasons and years (4:10). They are making much of their new teachers (4:17) by desiring to be under the law (4:21). This is really to submit to a yoke of bondage (5:1), if they receive circumcision (5:2–3 and 6:12). Thus they will end up biting and devouring each other (5:15).

The Opponents

1. The sources of the opposition:

"Troublers" are now perverting the gospel (1:7), preaching a contrary gospel in Galatia (1:8–9) by demanding circumcision (5:2 and 6:13). At the same time "false brethren" attacked Paul's freedom in Jerusalem (2:4–5) and "certain men from James" representing the circumcision party disputed Paul in Antioch (2:12–13).

2. The claims against Paul:

Paul is a man-pleaser (1:10). He preaches man's gospel, having received it from man (1:11–12). Conferring with flesh and blood, Paul is dependent upon Jerusalem (1:16–17). Titus was circumcised with Paul's consent (2:3) and many things were added to his gospel (2:6).

3. The nature of the opposition:

Opponents are subverting the Galatians, luring them back to observing days, months, seasons and years (4:10). They make much of them (4:17), seeking to put them under the law (5:1), and have them receive circumcision (5:2). They are hindering the Galatians (5:7–8), troublers (5:10), who are unsettling them (5:12). By compelling them to be circumcised they want to make a good showing in their flesh (6:12) but do not keep the whole law themselves (6:13).

4.

We are now ready to summarize Paul's reason for writing:

Paul's Reasons for Writing

(Now compare your answers with mine.)

Paul's Reasons for Writing

Paul writes Galatians to defend the church against "Christ plus." In this case his opponents propose Christ plus circumcision and keeping the Mosaic law. Legalism is one way of adding to the gospel which, centered in Christ alone, sets men free.

Since Paul founded these young churches, fake teachers have subverted the purity of his message and challenged his apostleship. They apparently claim that Paul is inconsistent in his preaching (cares nothing for truth) in order to make fast converts. Thus he preaches a popular, easy gospel unrelated to God's revelation to Israel in the Old Testament. Lacking continuity with the past, Paul also lacks continuity with the present, not being a true apostle. Subservient to the Jerusalem church, they claim, Paul is at odds with the preaching and practice of the "pillars" there. Either he is a "junior apostle" or none at all.

In light of this confusion the Galatians are falling for the arguments *for* the law and *against* Paul. They are attracted by the security of the past: the antiquity of Jewish ritual and regulation.

Thus Paul writes:

1. To reestablish his apostolic authority.
2. To defend the truth of his gospel.
3. To clarify his relationship with the Jerusalem church and pillar apostles.
4. To expose the bad theology and selfish motives of the legalists.
5. To call the church to its freedom in Christ and life in the Spirit.

SUMMARIZING GALATIANS

The thesis of this book appears in 1:11–12:

> For I would have you know, brethren, that the gospel preached by me is not man's gospel. For I did not receive it from man, nor was I taught it, but it came through a revelation of Jesus Christ.

Thus the truth of the gospel is defended:
1. Historically—1:1–2:14
2. Theologically—2:15–4:7
3. Personally—4:8–20
4. Allegorically—4:21–31
5. Practically——5:1–6:18

While the general movement is from history to theology to practical application, the specific movement is from experience to theological and historical understanding.

Paul begins with the Galatians' present experience:

"You are deserting" (1:6). He then shows them that this desertion is, in effect, the desertion of Christ himself (1:12) which is verified not only through Paul's conversion but also the confirmation of his ministry by the Jerusalem church. After this historical–theological defense against their treachery he returns in 3:1 to experience: "You are bewitched." The spell cast over them has led to forgetfulness about the gospel preached and the Spirit's work. Paul immediately grounds his assertion in the promise to Abraham and the curse of the law resolved in Christ. Thus most of chapter 3 through 4:7 is an historical–theological exposition of the true gospel which has produced authentic Christian experience. In 4:8 the Apostle returns to the present experience of the Galatians and reminds them of his past and present concern for them. Then off he goes again in a theological allegory based on Abraham and his two sons in 4:21–31.

Returning to their experience in chapter 5, Paul warns of the dangers and bitter fruit of legalism contrasted with life in the Spirit. Chapter 6 concludes his exhortation by the offering of his example: "let no man trouble me; for I bear on my body the marks of Jesus" (6:17). Thus starting where the Galatians are, and reminding them of what they have, Paul makes his history, theology and ethics live in a context of reality. While arguing, in part, from experience, the question is: what distinguishes true or false religious experience? Paul's touchstone is the gospel: Christ plus nothing.

THE STRUCTURE OF GALATIANS

This oversimplified diagram is designed to help us picture the book before us. The more we see it as a whole, the more the parts make sense.

Chapter 1	Chapter 2	Chapter 3	Chapter 4	Chapter 5	Chapter 6
1 SALUTATION Paul to Galatians	*1* Truth of Gospel defended in Jerusalem	*1* Experience Bewitched	*1* Assurance Son Heir	*1* Freedom Danger of circumcision	*1* Exhortation Burden-bearing
6 Experience Deserters		*6* Abraham Promise Law	*8* Danger—turning back	Love—Servants	Sowing
11 Thesis—Gospel by Revelation Historical Defense Conversion	*11* Truth of Gospel defended in Antioch Theology—justified by faith	Curse Christ—Takes Curse Fulfills Promise Purpose of Law FAITH	*12* Paul's first visit & present perplexity	*13* Spirit vs. Flesh	*11* Farewell Warning
			21 Abraham's two sons Slave and free		Glory in the cross
24	*21*	*29*	*31*	*26*	*18*

HISTORICAL		THEOLOGICAL		PRACTICAL

Part Two

The Text

Now that we have taken an overview of the Book of Galatians, have re-created the historical situations of Paul, the Galatians, and his opponents, and have established Paul's reasons for writing, we are now ready to turn to the text.

Remember the issue is "Christ plus." The essential truth of God's unconditional love, his accepting us just as we are, salvation being his work and his alone, the finality and supremacy of Jesus Christ—all of this and more is at stake. No wonder Paul comes out swinging. It is a matter of life and death—for eternity.

The Inductive Questions

As we turn to the text itself we will use six questions to uncover its meaning.

1. The Language Question

This question deals with the *definition of the words, vocabulary.* Do I understand each word in the paragraph? If not, I must look it up in a regular dictionary or a Bible dictionary. This question also deals with *style*— Is it poetry or prose? A letter, parable, or proverb? How is it being said? What is the form or sentence structure? Why are the particular words chosen? Where do they appear in the context? How often are they used?

2. The Historical Question

This question deals with the *setting of the text* and its historical content. Who is speaking or acting? What is being said of an historical nature? When is it happening? We have already dealt with this question at length in our previous study. This will just be a review.

3. The Theological Question

This question deals with the *theological content*. What truths are taught about the nature of God, man, sin, salvation, the church, the Christian life? How can we understand them systematically in this paragraph? How do they relate to the rest of the letter?

4. The Strategic Question

This question deals with *where a particular paragraph or idea fits* in light of Paul's *reasons for writing*. We have used a military metaphor to explain this. A commander creates a strategy and uses tactics to form his battle plan in winning a war. A coach creates a game plan to use his team effectively with the proper plays to win the game. A cook follows ordered steps in a recipe to reach the goal of the perfect cake. So Paul uses tactics in accomplishing his goals in writing his letter and we want to see *how* he does this—how one idea leads to the next in reaching his goal.

5. The Contemporary Question

This question deals with the *application* of the text to *our world today*. How do we apply what Paul has said to government, politics, economics, business, education, the institutional church, the assumptions, values and goals of our society? What is the social application of the text?

6. The Personal Question

This question deals with the *application* of the text to *our own lives* today. How do we apply what Paul has said to our personalities, needs, families, close friends, moral decisions, goals? This is the question of discipleship: What am I going to do about what I have learned?

We shall now try to apply all of these questions to Galatians. Sometimes one or more of them may not fit. Do not force yourself to write something. Meditate on the passage—more may come later. A study sheet is provided. You may make your own for your notebook following this sample.

INDUCTIVE QUESTIONS FOR —————————— ——————————
                                                Book   Chapter & Verse

1. Language:

2. Historical:

3. Theological:

4. Strategic:

5. Contemporary:

6. Personal:

1

Galatians

1:1-2

1 Paul an apostle—not from men nor through man, but through Jesus Christ and God the Father, who raised him from the dead—² and all the brethren who are with me,
To the churches of Galatia:

1. Language

VOCABULARY—An *apostle* is one who is sent with a commission. Jesus appointed twelve (Mark 3:14). Judas was replaced with one who had shared in Jesus' earthly ministry and witnessed the resurrection (Acts 1:21–22). Paul's claim to apostleship is based on his being a resurrection witness also (1 Cor. 15:8, cf. 1 Cor. 9:1–2). Here in Galatians, Paul specifically anchors his apostleship in the risen Christ (1:1). *Galatia,* a province in Asia Minor, which is in the central part of modern Turkey.

STYLE—1:1–2 is a salutation—"Paul . . . to the churches." Obviously, here, Paul uses this structure to identify himself, robed in his authority, to the Galatians.

2. **Historical**—Paul is an apostle by the direct action of Jesus Christ and God the Father. He writes surrounded by traveling companions who share his viewpoint. The Apostle addresses several congregations in Galatia which suggests that the letter will be circulated among them and be devoid of personal notes fitting for one congregation.

3. **Theological**—Paul opens Galatians using the salutation to define

his authority. It is the highest. Lacking a human source ("not from men") and lacking human mediation ("nor through man"), it comes directly from Jesus Christ and God the Father. Paul adds, "who raised him from the dead," suggesting that it is the risen Christ who has called and commissioned him as an apostle. Thus, Paul is implicitly an eyewitness to the resurrection as are the original twelve. This is the heart of his authority. In establishing his position, Paul also gives us the highest picture of Jesus Christ. Christ is not on the side of man ("not from men nor through man"), but God ("but through Jesus Christ and God the Father"). Jesus is divine. He stands with God the Father; he shares the Father's work—in this case in calling apostles. Here is a part of the raw material for our doctrine of the deity of Christ. Furthermore, both the Father and the Son relate to each other as they function together. Later, with the addition of the Holy Spirit, this developed into the doctrine of the Trinity. While Paul stresses Jesus' deity, this Jesus was also human, he died a real death and was raised *by the Father,* suggesting his subordination to and dependence upon the Father. Thus, this verse establishes:

1. The deity of Christ.
2. The unity of the Father and Son in nature.
3. The humanity of Christ.
4. The subordination of the Son to the Father in function.

4. Strategic—Paul no sooner opens up Galatians than he runs up his flag asking the churches to salute. He arrests them and flashes his badge. Here are his apostolic credentials. The challenge to Paul from his opponents centers, in part, in the claim that he is an inferior apostle. Paul will have nothing of it. Peter laid no hands on his head. There was no election held in Jerusalem for Paul. It was Christ himself, the risen Lord, who appeared to him and commissioned him. Ultimate authority rests in God the Father who raising Christ from the dead shared in Paul's call.

Thus the Galatians and their opponents have to do with Paul, the direct ambassador of Jesus Christ, no one else. The Apostle's opening is designed to overwhelm the Galatians with the divine claim—to deal with Paul is to deal with Christ himself.

5. Contemporary—Paul presses us immediately with the question of authority. There is the authority of reason, the authority of tradition, the authority of institutions. There is the authority of wisdom, the authority of experience, the authority of power. Paul claims direct, divine authority. How are we to weigh his claim? In a relativistic, rationalistic, and pragmatic age it sounds so mystical, so dogmatic, so supernatural. After we have locked God out of his universe by the closed system of the scientific world view, he is suddenly back. As C. S. Lewis remarks, a game of cops and robbers is fun in a dark house until a real footfall is heard on the stairs—then it's all for real. This is Paul's claim—it's all for real—Christ has been raised from the dead. Paul has been empowered by him to represent his interests to us. What will we do with that? Is it possible in this letter that we will hear the divine footfall on our stairs? More than possible—probable, even certain.

6. **Personal**—Paul is unafraid to present himself in his divine authority. Have I allowed God to so grip my heart? While I am no apostle in the technical sense, is it not true that Christ has called me? Have I not felt his risen touch? If so, why am I so afraid, so unwilling to stand boldly for him? I find myself so "other-directed" in David Reisman's terms, so dependent upon what others think and say. I seem constantly to need human approval—when will divine approval be enough? When will I cry with Luther, "Here I stand, I can do no other"? Paul has been humbled by Christ so that he can stand stoutly before men. If I were really secure before God would I not enjoy that same freedom in this world? Perhaps Paul gives me another secret here—he has brethren with him who share his ministry and call. I do not have to go it alone. If I discover the "brethren with me" I can be Christ's person in the world. Today I must open my heart to a brother.

Galatians
1:3-5

> 3 Grace to you and peace from God the Father and our Lord Jesus Christ, ⁴ who gave himself for our sins to deliver us from the present evil age, according to the will of our God and Father; ⁵ to whom be the glory for ever and ever. Amen.

1. Language

VOCABULARY—*Grace:* God's mercy toward us, "his grace . . . a gift" (Romans 3:24). *Peace:* the end of our warfare against God, "so making peace . . . (he) might reconcile us both to God in one body through the cross, thereby bringing the hostility to an end" (Ephesians 2:15–16). *Sins:* the repeated failure to live up to God's character, "all have sinned and fall short of the glory of God" (Romans 3:23).

STYLE—The style of these verses is formal. Paul uses the blessing, "Grace to you and peace," as the vehicle for introducing the heart of his gospel in the next verse. The sentence ends in a liturgical ascription to God, "to whom be the glory for ever and ever. Amen." Such solemn language would not fail to impress the Galatians with the seriousness of Paul's thought. God as Father is mentioned twice (also see 1:1), Paul stresses this aspect of God by repetition.

2. Historical—There is no specific history here which deals with Paul, the Galatians, or the opponents, although the theological content relates to the attack on Paul.

3. Theological—Paul gives the standard blessing of "grace and peace." These are both salvation words. Grace is God's free forgiveness, unearned and undeserved by us. Peace is God's *Shalom*, God's wholeness. When our warfare against him ends objectively, we are put back together subjectively. What happens for us—peace accomplished on the cross, now happens in us—peace in our hearts. The objects of grace and peace are the Christians, "to you." The sources of grace and peace are "God the Father and our Lord Jesus Christ." Once again, as the Father and the Son share in Paul's authority (1:1), so they share in the working of salvation. Here, however, rather than stressing the resurrection of Christ which is crucial for Paul's apostleship, the death of Christ is central, which is crucial for salvation. The elaboration in 1:4 allows the Apostle to establish that Christ freely "gave himself" for, on behalf of, our sins and the result is deliverance from this present evil age. In other words, the result is freedom from the world's false value system which holds us in bondage. All of this transpired by the will of "our God and Father." In stressing the Fatherhood of God, Paul shows that our salvation means that we are in God's family, at home in the universe, and that Jesus' teaching us to pray "our Father" is now essential to the way Paul views God. To be delivered from this present evil age is to be delivered into the eternal arms of love: God is our Father. Paul ascribes glory to God in worship and ends with the finality of *Amen*. Nothing more can be added to the reality of salvation.

4. Strategic—As Paul has stressed his authority, which is under attack, in the salutation, so now he stresses his message, which is under attack, in the blessing. He no sooner begins this letter than he calls the churches to salute him and reminds them of the heart of his gospel— the cancellation of sin and our deliverance from this world's bondage.

We see here how Paul uses the traditional letter form to alert the Galatians to his basic thrust. He is now saying, in effect, "These themes are so crucial that I can hardly wait to get them before you." Thus, the salutation and blessing are not incidental to the letter, but put Paul immediately on the offensive–defensive with two bold statements about his authority and message. In this letter we are at the heart of all that counts for Paul.

5. Contemporary—This age is in many respects so attractive that we recoil against Paul's designation of it as "evil." Our materialism and sensuality make us fat and dull. "How can this age be evil?" we ask from the stupor of our false radiance. How seduced we are! "The present evil age" is so evil because it is so deceptive. When man had to fight the elements and fear the plague he knew the age was evil as a sheer physical fact. Our uneasiness in the recent "energy crisis" helps us now to understand this. "The present evil age" shows its colors to us in its false assumptions: man's goodness and the reign of science and technology; in its false values: selfishness and competition; and in its false goals: material success, the control of power, social acceptance.

To be delivered from this bondage is a greater reality than escape from physical disaster could ever be. Such deliverance is possible only through a total personality reorientation—accomplished morally for us in Christ's self-giving for sin and accomplished existentially for us when we receive him, the Eternal One, who breaks our bondage to the transitory decay of the world's passing show.

When so many false deliverances are being offered today—astrology, eastern mysticism, chanting, psychoanalysis, drugs, alcohol, religion, education, and political revolution, we must, with Paul, offer the true deliverance based in Christ's cross, giving both a moral solution to our sense of separation and personal reorientation: "our Lord Jesus Christ, who gave himself for our sins to deliver us from the present evil age. . . ."

6. Personal—I struggle to be delivered, to accept my deliverance. For ten years I served a large "successful" church. Its success was often measured in the size of its physical plant, the number of its members and the growth of its budget. As long as I was "packing them in" I was held to be successful, my job was secure. Much of my life, especially in the early years of my ministry, was dominated by the values of "this present evil age," embodied in the church. The demand for success and the insecurities of my struggle for self-acceptance united to produce a huge amount of effort in ministry to somehow fulfill the expectations of the church. When good-looking athletes and sorority girls attended the college department where I ministered, the adults were proud of me. When, however, long-haired hippies in Levis and workshirts began to attend they were not so sure. When blacks began to come to the church, fears were aroused.

At the same time, I was tempted to judge my success by money. Again, in the early years, I was paid minimally. How easily I fell to the temptation of locating my value in my paycheck. "Today I'm worth $125.00" was what I, in effect, said. Then resentment sprang up as I compared myself with better paid staff members. In the Presbyterian Church we talk of the equality of the clergy. I viewed that with cynicism.

Since the church appeared to value itself in terms of numbers and budget I absorbed the same standards for myself. All of this only reflected the larger culture. A successful business is measured by production and sales: so the church, so the clergy, so me.

But Christ has come to deliver me from all of this. If we value Jesus' ministry by numbers, he died a failure. Is it possible that God prefers quality to quantity? Can I follow the son of Man who had nowhere to lay his head (Matthew 8:20)? The church for me today is not merely a building or budget, but a body of people committed to Christ and to each other—this is the beginning of my deliverance.

Galatians
1:6–9

6 I am astonished that you are so quickly deserting him who called you in the grace of Christ and turning to a different gospel—7 not that there is another gospel, but there are some who trouble you and want to pervert the gospel of Christ. 8 But even if we, or an angel from heaven, should preach to you a gospel contrary to that which we preached to you, let him be accursed. 9 As we have said before, so now I say again, If any one is preaching to you a gospel contrary to that which you received, let him be accursed.

1. Language

VOCABULARY—*Gospel* is a key word repeated five times. It means "good news." This includes both event, "news," and interpretation, "good." Thus the Christian proclamation is that through the death and resurrection of Jesus Christ (event), sins are forgiven (interpretation, see 1 Cor. 15:1–4).

STYLE—The surprising and startling thing about this paragraph is that in it Paul breaks the normal letter form. Usually he would follow the salutation and blessing with a prayer of thanksgiving. Here, however, he omits it, as if to say, "I have nothing to be thankful for over you." This shattering of his style would jolt the Galatians like a misplaced chord jolts the music lover. Added to this is the emotion and even violence of Paul's words: "I am astonished," "you are deserting," "let him be accursed." Note also the repetition in 1:9, "As we have said before, so now I say again." This makes Paul's conclusion doubly emphatic. We know he means what he says.

2. Historical

—Paul reveals his relationship to the Galatians here; he was the evangelist who founded the church (1:8). They received the gospel (1:9). Now, however, they are "quickly deserting" God himself (1:6). As new Christians, they have been seduced by "some who trouble you" (1:7), who pervert the gospel of Christ. Paul is astonished at all of this (1:6), expressing his dismay in turbulent language. Now we see why he has stated his authority and message in 1:1–5; the very truth of the gospel is at stake in his churches.

3. Theological

—God has called the Galatians "in the grace of Christ" (1:6). The sign of that grace which God initiates has been Paul's coming as their evangelist and their reception of his message. For the Apostle there is only one gospel—all the rest are perversions. Like the character in Bunyan's *Pilgrim's Progress*, he is "valiant for truth." The ultimate issue for him is not evangelistic success, or subjective religious experience, or institutional growth, or even psychological health, but *truth*. When the truth of the gospel is at stake, Paul's nerve center has been hit.

Those who turn to another gospel are "deserters." Those who proclaim another gospel are "perverters."

Paul is indifferent to his own position in Galatia. He is so adamant for the truth that he can write, "even if we, or an angel from heaven, should preach to you a gospel contrary to that which we preached to you, let him be accursed" (1:8). If he returned with another message, he would want to be cast out. Moreover, even an angel, a supernatural revelation, should be rejected if it contradicts the truth. For Paul there is no Hegelian dialectic, no synthesis of opposites, no Eastern assimilation of polarities. There is only truth, the revealed gospel, in whose light all alternatives are falsehoods. Here is the offense of the particular. Here is the exclusiveness of the Christian claim—one gospel. So let it be.

4. **Strategic**—Paul, as noted above, begins with a blast—no thanksgiving is possible under the circumstances of the Galatians' desertion. The formalities of the salutation and blessing being over, the Apostle explodes in amazement that the churches could turn from God's call "in the grace of Christ" to any alternative message. They are accepting a "different gospel" but, Paul quickly corrects himself, there is only one gospel. Nothing else can be compared to it. It stands in a unique position, in a category all of its own. Thus the perversions are shams, "not that there is another gospel."

The letter begins, therefore, with Paul plunging into the center of the issue. He expresses his feelings about the Galatians' apostasy. As he begins with himself and their behavior, his theology is not abstract; it arises out of the crisis of the confrontation.

Paul is obviously building on his apostolic authority. He is appealing both emotionally and conceptually as he expresses his anguish and states the exclusiveness of his message as a thesis yet to be defended. Thus we rightly expect to find in this letter the mind of Paul wrestling with the truth and the heart of Paul wrestling with his converts. This beginning shows him adamant and angry: those who pervert the truth should be cursed and cast out. To use a military analogy, Paul launches a surprise attack, ripping down the Galatians' defenses. It is a mental and emotional blitz. The best defense is a good offense and Paul has immediately seized it.

5. **Contemporary**—We live in an age inundated by religion. Not only is there a babel of competing Christian groups but also an ever widening offer of spiritual alternatives. Eastern holy men claim to be equal to Jesus Christ as God's living revelation. Cults present new prophets raised up in the latter days to reform or renew the church. Books are promised to bring illuminating revelations with "keys" to the scriptures. If we follow the predictions of our astrological signs or chant a mysterious formula we are assured the fulfillment of our every desire. The organization and zealousness of these groups are impressive.

Some display admirable family life and high morality. The glow of their converts apparently rivals the best Christian experience. Often our churches are drab and harmless in comparison. It seems that there are many new "angels from heaven." How, then, do we work our way through all these claims and counter-claims?

Paul gives us a clue: test the way these groups stand up to the gospel. If the gospel is unique, then what do they say to it? Finally, the test of true religious experience must be that it comes from a true source. Satan can perform miracles. He counterfeits God's Messiah. The gospel defines the truth of God which must be the test of true religion. Thus we must know this gospel and apply it as the unerring standard for that which will not only open heaven's door but fill our lives with present meaning.

6. Personal—Paul's intolerance is certainly out of step with the spirit of the age. I must ask myself, is there anything worth getting mad about? Or better yet, what would I die for? A young Christian comes to me announcing that he is joining a cult. A waitress tells me she used to attend our church, but now is into "spiritism." As I watch people seduced what is my reaction?

How also do I square what Paul says here with Jesus' command to love our enemies (Matthew 5:44)? Does this command turn me into a wet noodle? I do notice this—Paul is at white-heat against those who have infiltrated the Christian fellowship to lead it astray. In our community we must be defensive for our converts, protecting new and unstable Christians. At the same time, with grace, we must proclaim God's truth in the world. C. S. Lewis evidenced charm, sophistication, and humor as he commended the truth of the gospel to modern man.

Paul seems to approach each situation uniquely. He is willing to call wavering new Christians into account and so must I. Is it really being intolerant to pull someone out of the fire to keep him from burning to death?

Galatians
1:10

10 Am I now seeking the favor of men, or of God? Or am I trying to please men? If I were still pleasing men, I should not be a servant of Christ.

1. Language

VOCABULARY—Paul defines himself here as a servant, or literally a *slave* of Christ. Here is a picture of bondage and obedience to another. Paradoxically, Paul's slavery has made him a free man.

STYLE—This paragraph contains rhetorical questions which imply their answer and then a concluding statement.

2. Historical—By Paul's defense against "seeking the favor of men," "trying to please men," and "still pleasing man," we can infer that exactly this charge has been brought against him by his opponents. They have told the Galatians, "Paul does not really care for the truth. If he did he would have instructed you in the law. His real concern is to make quick converts and to have showy success. By lifting the offense of the Old Testament law and circumcision from you, you have received only half the truth, cheap grace. Thus you cannot trust Paul's motives or message." This charge has been refuted in the previous paragraph by Paul's adamant stand for the truth, and on this basis he now shows that rather than pleasing man, his passion is to please Christ.

3. Theological—For Paul as his apostleship is either human or divine (1:1), so his life will be lived either for man or God. The basic contrast is between pleasing men or serving Christ. Either we will live an outer-directed life, seeking our security and acceptance from the world; or an inner-directed life receiving our security and acceptance from God. In terms of basic motivation, we cannot have it both ways. We live determined by the world or by Christ.

It is one thing to *seek* the favor of men and to *try* to please men and another actually to do so. By stressing the motivation in "seeking" and "trying" Paul contrasts his goal from that of a worldly man. The paradox of the Christian life is that a man pleasing God will often please men, not because that is the controlling goal of his life, but because in his pleasing God, love for men and integrity of life become natural results. The man free from himself and others, secure in God's love, is best able to meet the needs around him in a way not dominated by possessiveness and the fear of rejection.

4. Strategic—This brief paragraph really completes the previous one. Paul's passion for the truth demonstrates his commitment not to please men, but to serve Christ. Rhetorical questions thrust the thought home with emotional punch. After this shock treatment, the Apostle is ready to make his carefully reasoned defense. Disarmed and reeling by a forced opening, Paul brings up his historical and theological reinforcements to attack us.

5. **Contemporary**—The church is always caught in the tension—pleasing men or God. How easy it is to justify pleasing men for the sake of evangelism or apologetics or just sheer survival. Intellectually, Rudolf Bultmann felt it necessary to jettison the miracles of the Bible because they offended the scientific assumptions of modern man. The established church in Germany easily capitulated to Hitler so that she would not lose her "influence." A theological student proposed to Dietrich Bonhoeffer that by joining the State Church, he would have access to influential pulpits. Bonhoeffer replied, "One act of obedience is worth a thousand sermons." It is that one act of obedience, however, that is so costly in our age as well. How many pastors have lost their pulpits for welcoming blacks into their congregations? How many pastors have refused to build new institutional monuments to themselves as proof of their success? How many laymen have been willing to stem the tide of dishonesty in business, thereby suffering financial loss? Can we sign our name to Paul's motto: "If I were still pleasing men, I should not be a servant of Christ"?

6. **Personal**—The theme of "pleasing men" hits me at my most vulnerable point. Perhaps my greatest fear is the fear of rejection. I expend tremendous amounts of emotional energy to avoid it. I will feel people out carefully so as not to offend them. The experiences of rejection which I have had are "death" experiences. I once asked a girl to marry me and she refused. I was shattered for a long time.

Now Christ comes and asks for my allegiance. What is to be the goal of my life? Seeking the favor of God? Serving Christ? I may suffer misunderstanding and even rejection. Yes, but if I seek the favor of God, I will be free at last not only to serve Christ, but also to serve men as they need to be served and not as I need to serve them.

Galatians
1:11–17

11 For I would have you know, brethren, that the gospel which was preached by me is not man's

gospel. [12] For I did not receive it from man, nor was I taught it, but it came through a revelation of Jesus Christ. [13] For you have heard of my former life in Judaism, how I persecuted the church of God violently and tried to destroy it; [14] and I advanced in Judaism beyond many of my own age among my people, so extremely zealous was I for the traditions of my fathers. [15] But when he who had set me apart before I was born, and had called me through his grace, [16] was pleased to reveal his Son 'to me, in order that I might preach him among the Gentiles, I did not confer with flesh and blood, [17] nor did I go up to Jerusalem to those who were apostles before me, but I went away into Arabia; and again I returned to Damascus.

1. Language

VOCABULARY—Simple and clear. Jerusalem is the capital of Palestine. Arabia is the desert east of Damascus, Damascus itself being the ancient capital of the Nabataean Kingdom and the modern capital of Syria.

STYLE—Closely argued history. Notice the use of *I* in 1:13–14 and *he* and *his* in 1:15–16 and then *I* in 1:15–17. In the midst of the *I* of Paul's life, God, *he* intervened. This is the point of this essential paragraph.

2. Historical—Paul's thesis is clear and it is the heart of the letter: the gospel came not through any human mediation, but through a revelation of Jesus Christ (1:12). He defends this thesis by reference to history: *before* and *after*.

The "before" is Paul's life in Judaism. It was exhibited by zeal and action, "I persecuted the church of God" and study, "I advanced in Judaism beyond many of my own age . . . so extremely zealous was I for the traditions of my fathers" (1:14). While living at the cultural heart of Judaism, Paul received the revelation of Christ.

The *after* stresses God's grace operative throughout Paul's life. The most extreme expression of it appears in 1:15—he was set apart for God before his birth. This became effective in his call "through his grace" when God's Son was revealed to Paul. The purpose of it all was that he might preach Christ among the Gentiles. Thus the Apostle turns from the "I" of Judaism to the "he" of Christianity that he might discover a new "I" centered in Christ and invested in the world.

This is followed by a defense against the charge that Paul's apostleship has come from human mediation. As he has stated positively, all has been in the hands of God—his message, his call, his commission. Now he specifically denies any human consultation ("I did not confer with flesh and blood"), or relationship with the Jerusalem apostles. Paul was separated by grace and geography. His time was consumed in Arabia and then again in Damascus. Note that the "again" in 1:17 implies that Paul had been in Damascus previously as confirmed by Acts 9:8.

Here, then, we have a classic example of Paul's personal witness. His history justifies his thesis that his apostleship and gospel came directly from God.

3. Theological—Paul's apostleship is not from man (1:1), Paul's purpose in life is not to please man (1:10), and now Paul's gospel is not "man's gospel" (1:11). Here is the claim for direct, divine revelation and it is the thesis heart of Galatians.

Paul presents his disclaimers. He did not receive his gospel from man (source) nor was he taught it by man (means), but it came through a revelation of Jesus Christ (1:12).

Revelation for Paul is God's direct invasion of his life. The word means an apocalypse, a "lifting of the veil." Nowhere does the Apostle suggest prior conditioning through dissatisfaction with Jewish legalism or moral conflict over persecuting the church. To the contrary, in the midst of a zealous, pious life, Christ came. This not only guarantees the nature of Paul's gospel as revelation, but also the substance of Paul's gospel as grace. He was arrested in the midst of his persecution by the one he rejected and opposed. Paul sees this intervention as God's election before his birth. How could he have merited or earned such grace if he was marked out from his mother's womb? Since the call came in the midst of Paul's violent opposition to the church, it was indeed a call "through his grace." And what was the substance of this call, this revelation of Jesus Christ? It was "his Son to me," or as the RSV footnote points out, literally, "his Son in me."

Paul's movement from Judaism to Christ was the movement from performance to a person; from tradition outside to Christ inside; from religious to spiritual life. And what is the key? "His Son in me." Call it mysticism, call it supernaturalism, call it what you will, but the heart of Paul's evangelical faith is that the risen, living Christ now lives in him. In Judaism Paul had a great system of religious performance. In Christianity Paul found the intimacy of Christ's presence residing in his body.

But this revelation, this overwhelming spiritual experience was no mere subjective flash. The entrance of Christ into Paul was a crucial part of God's plan for him even before his birth. It also carried with it content—the revelation of the gospel. Thus as Christ came to Paul (1:16), so also the good news of and about Christ came as well (1:11–12).

The Apostle beautifully unites objective truth and subjective experience. He was encountered by a person calling him into the deepest relationship possible, and at the same time that person was and is true. The nature of Paul's relationship with him is defined by the gospel which also came in the revelation of Jesus Christ himself (1:11–12).

What did Paul learn in his conversion? With Christian blood on his hands he discovered that grace and forgiveness are free and unmerited. He also learned that Christ was alive, not locked into history. Paul learned as well that in the gift of the truth of Christ came the summons to preach Christ. If Christ's mercy was really free, then the Gentiles too must be the object of it (1:16). All of this sent Paul, not into conference, but into retreat to Arabia. What a massive reorientation must now take place in his mind and heart.

Paul's claim to apostleship and to revelation must be accepted or rejected. If accepted (and how else could his experience be explained?) we have in him a primary witness to the meaning of Christ for us.

As the Apostle moved from religion (Judaism) to revelation (Christ) so, in our own ways, must we. It is in the authenticity of his spiritual life and not in his apostolic authority that we have a direct model for our own confrontation with Jesus Christ.

Paul has spoken of God as Father (1:1, 3, 4); now he speaks of Christ as Son (1:16). Christ is God's unique Son as we are not. What does Paul mean by "Son"? C. S. Lewis is helpful. He remarks that as a human son shares human nature, so the divine Son shares the divine nature. Thus when Paul calls Christ "Son," he means that he stands in the most intimate, personal, and substantial relation to the Father. It is this Son who lives his divine life in and through Paul.

4. Strategic—The Apostle now presents the first part of his defense against his opponents. That his gospel came by a revelation of Christ is proven by the impossibility of its coming any other way because of his zealous life as a Jew. He was no marginal figure, culturally alienated, restless for some new religious experience. Not only is Paul's argument effective against a false psychologizing of his condition, it is also devastating as it anticipates the legalists who are troubling the Galatians.

In effect Paul says, "So you are tempted to submit yourselves to the law and receive circumcision? Well, I did all of that. In fact I was more of a legalist than my opponents could ever dream of being. It was all to no avail. That was my former life (1:13). At best, it was an imperfect stage along the way. Now that Christ has come all of this has been left behind. Would you Galatians go back to that which I have left? Would you progress in the faith by returning to my past? How absurb."

As his first point, then, Paul demonstrates that his gospel came by the direct revelation of Christ, and in his argument he shows the foolishness of the Galatians embracing what he has abandoned. As his second point, Paul answers the charge of dependence upon human authority. He did no apostle visiting to secure approval for his call (1:16–17). The grace and power of Christ were enough. Paul is an apostle by divine appointment; he ranks with the rest and the best.

5. Contemporary—This passage raises the issue of the supernatural in the church and culture. Do we have room today in the church for the sovereign intervention of God? How easy it is to become the prisoner of our tradition. The "Judaism" of the church cannot allow God to intervene. It is not just sophisticated to disbelieve in the supernatural, it is also safe. We do not have to fear the living God. The neo-Pentecostal movement in Protestant and Catholic churches, while excessive theologically and experientially at times, is a valid protest against locking God out of the church through tradition. Why should not the "order of service" be upset? Where is the freedom and power of Christ clearly demonstrated?

For our culture this passage becomes an embarrassment to those who reject the faith on naturalistic grounds. Not only does Paul offer no historical basis to psychologize his conversion, he offers proof that it cannot be done. We accept or reject his claim; we cannot rationalize it. The challenge to the closed universe of the scientific world view comes from many quarters. More and more people are experiencing the supernatural. While this can be demonic it also opens the door to Christ. No longer can Paul's conversion be shrugged off. It could happen to us too.

6. Personal—I must take my stand with Paul here; I too have a "before" and "after." My "former life" was in religion: a liberal Protestant moralism. The emphasis was not on God, but me. But the bland nature of my religion led neither to the persecution of my opponents, nor to the zeal for my traditions. I became a church drop-out.

Christ encountered me through an organization called "Young Life" in high school. At the time of my conversion I would have stressed how I had come to the point of accepting Christ. Later I stressed how Christ led me to that point. More and more am I conscious, as was Paul, that it is all of grace.

Unlike Paul, the revelation of Jesus to me was mediated through Scripture and demonstrated in the lives of Christian friends. This, however, does not make its reality any less. Paul stands in a unique position as apostle because of Christ's direct intervention in his life. Paul and I and all believers share in the common experience of Christ in our lives.

The Apostle sees the purpose of his salvation in preaching to the Gentiles. I can identify specifically with that too. Moreover, all Christians are in some sense communicators. Good news must be shared—that is its nature. Christ calls us to himself to invest us in the world. As Dr. Robert Munger says, "When you get close to the heart of Christ, you get close to what is on his heart—people." It is to people, then, that we must go.

Galatians
1:18–24

18 Then after three years I went up to Jerusalem to visit Cephas, and remained with him fifteen days. [19] But I saw none of the other apostles except James the Lord's brother. [20] (In what I am writing to you, before God, I do not lie!) [21] Then I went into the regions of Syria and Cilicia. [22] And I was still not known by sight to the churches of Christ in Judea; [23] they only heard it said, "He who once persecuted us is now preaching the faith he once tried to destroy." [24] And they glorified God because of me.

1. Language

VOCABULARY—*Jerusalem*, which has already appeared in 1:17 and will appear in 2:1, appears here. Obviously Paul's relation to Jerusalem, the capital city of Palestine, is crucial. Also *Cephas* appears here as well as in 2:1, 11, and 14. *Cephas* is the Greek transliteration for the Aramaic word *Rock*. *Peter* is the English transliteration for the Greek word *Rock*.

Paul uses them interchangeably in chapter 2 as the name of Christ's chief apostle.

James "the Lord's brother" is distinguished from James the brother of John who was executed by Herod Agrippa I (Acts 12:1–2).

Syria and *Cilicia* are lands bordering the northeast Mediterranean, modern Syria and Turkey. *Tarsus* is Paul's hometown (Acts 22:3) in Cilicia. *Judea* is the southern part of Palestine.

STYLE—As Paul continues his historical argument he punctuates with the use of *then* in 1:18 and 21 (also 2:1). He is careful to include places, names, and time sequences. The oath in 1:20, "In what I am writing to you, before God, I do not lie!" confirms that Paul's chronicle is in answer to his opponents.

2. **Historical**—Paul's absence from Jerusalem is resolved "after three years" when he finally visits for the first time since his conversion (1:18). Whether the "after three years" refers to his becoming a Christian or his return to Damascus is not clear. The purpose of his visit is specifically to see Cephas, the leader of the Jerusalem church and the chief apostle. Peter and Paul are together for about two weeks; James the Lord's brother is the only other apostle seen at that time, and Paul confirms this with an oath (1:20). After this Paul returned to his home territory in Syria and Cilicia apparently for at least a decade (see 2:1). His independence from Jerusalem is also seen in his absence from the surrounding Judean churches.

3. **Theological**—While Paul affirms his distinction from Jerusalem and the other apostles, he now confirms some contact with them. His direct call and reception of the gospel has neither launched him as the founder of a new religion nor even as the leader of a Christian sect. He is separate from Jerusalem and Peter, yet wedded to them. This tension in Galatians is often overlooked. Paul's relationship with Peter in no way compromises the uniqueness of his apostleship, but it does confirm the reality of his apostleship (see especially 2:1–10).

Undoubtedly Paul recounted his conversion and ministry to Peter, and Peter confirmed that the same Jesus who had discipled him had changed Paul. If this had not been the case Paul would never have returned to Jerusalem again as reported in 2:1–10. Thus the historical Jesus of Peter's experience was confirmed to be the same as the exalted Jesus of Paul's experience. The continuity between the historical Jesus and exalted Lord is guaranteed in the relationship between Peter and

Paul. C. H. Dodd remarks that when Peter and Paul met in Jerusalem they hardly talked about the weather for two weeks! Undoubtedly Paul peppered Peter with questions about his life with the earthly Lord. Paul forged a link with James the Lord's brother at that time which would also confirm the authenticity of his conversion to the real Christ.

Thus, while we must, like Paul, meet Jesus personally, we must be certain that the Jesus whom we have met is the Christ of the historic faith. The test, again, is not merely experience. The test is our continuity with the Biblical faith carried on in the life of the church. We must all go to our Jerusalem. In this sense, confirmation does not give faith, but it can assist in the assurance of faith.

The results of Paul's conversion are not only confirmation, but the worship and praise of God. "The persecutor has turned preacher," says the report in Judea, "and they glorified God because of me" (1:24). Our testimony rightly given turns hearts not to us, but to God. This is the test of witness "in the Spirit."

4. Strategic—As the oath confirms, "In what I am writing to you, before God, I do not lie!" (1:20), Paul continues his polemic history answering his opponents.

His independence from Jerusalem is demonstrated by the three-year lapse before his first Christian visit. Then his stay there was only for fifteen days with Peter and James, the Lord's brother. While these key figures in early Christianity undoubtedly shared much concerning Christ, Paul was long established in his own faith. After that he returned to his "home territory" and was not seen again even in Judea, much less Jerusalem.

In all this Paul demonstrates his independent conversion, his unique apostleship, his center of ministry in Damascus, Arabia, and later Syria and Cilicia, and his single contact with Jerusalem in, at least, a fourteen-year period (see 2:1).

It is Paul's purpose to downplay his time with Peter and James, yet that contact built the foundation for his unity with the earliest disciples of Jesus and his later reception in Jerusalem (2:1–10). What Paul suggests here and confirms later is that his welcome in Jerusalem is as a fellow apostle, not as a subordinate missionary who simplified the gospel for selfish gain.

5. Contemporary—The greatness of evangelical Christianity is its stress on a personal encounter with Jesus Christ, a genuine conversion experience. The danger of evangelical Christianity is excessive individualism. Paul holds the tension here. While his faith is uniquely personal, it is not unrelated to those in Christ before him. The first chapter of Galatians suggests two tests for authentic Christian experience—the standard, first, of the gospel, and, second, of the Christian community. Only when the second criterion has been applied as well as the first can I be evidenced as holding the full apostolic faith.

6. Personal—In my own experience the confirmation of my faith took place when I joined a historic church with a full body of believers. I was told in my early Christian life that I was merely going through a phase, that I would soon grow out of it. Surrounded by other high school Christians as I was, that charge sounded plausible. Then I began to attend a church and met grey-haired grandmothers who loved the Jesus I loved. "Some phase," I thought, "these old ladies are still in it." Only in the full fellowship of believers, young and old, rich and poor, black, brown, yellow, red and white shall we find the full assurance of our gospel confirmed in the totality of human life.

Questions for Discussion and Reflection: Chapter 1

1:1-2

1. What is my earliest experience of "authority"?
2. What authorities do I respect in my life today? What one symbol of authority is the most impressive to me? Why?
3. Who do I exercise authority over? How do I use this authority?
4. How do people feel about my authority?
5. What is "spiritual authority?" How should it be used?

1:3-5

6. How do I react to the word *bondage?* What was my biggest fear from ages 1-12? 13-18? 19-25? 26 to the present?
7. How have I been delivered from my bondages? Who has God used in my life to set me free? Share an example.
8. How has the gospel become my own "good news?"

1:6-9

9. Who are the biggest competitors today for my Christian attention?
10. "Every heresy represents a need not met by the church." How do I react to that statement?

11. How can I love people yet oppose their ideas? How do I feel when someone rejects my ideas? When am I the most open to change?

1:10

12. How do I feel about rejection? Share an experience where you have had to deal with it. How have you overcome?
13. "Every day we seek the favor of men." How can I illustrate this from my own experience? Is this good or bad?

1:11–17

14. What is my "former life in Judaism," my *before?*
15. What was the turning point for me?
16. How can I best describe my new life in Christ?
17. What has been God's purpose in saving me? Be specific.

1:18–24

18. With whom have I shared my faith?
19. Who has confirmed my belonging to Christ?
20. With what concrete body of believers am I identified?
21. Why did the early Christians have a hard time accepting Paul? Why would Christians have a hard time accepting me? What should this teach me?

2
Galatians
2:1-10

2 Then after fourteen years I went up again to Jerusalem with Barnabas, taking Titus along with me. [2] I went up by revelation; and I laid before them (but privately before those who were of repute) the gospel which I preach among the Gentiles, lest somehow I should be running or had run in vain. [3] But even Titus, who was with me, was not compelled to be circumcised, though he was a Greek. [4] But because of false brethren secretly brought in, who slipped in to spy out our freedom which we have in Christ Jesus, that they might bring us into bondage—[5] to them we did not yield submission even for a moment, that the truth of the gospel might be preserved for you. [6] And from those who were reputed to be something (what they were makes no difference to me; God shows no partiality)—those, I say, who were of repute added nothing to me; [7] but on the contrary, when they saw that I had been entrusted with the gospel to the uncircumcised, just as Peter had been entrusted with the gospel to the circumcised [8] (for he who worked through Peter for the mission to the circumcised worked through me also for the Gentiles), [9] and when they perceived the grace that was given to me, James and Cephas and John, who were reputed to be pillars, gave to me and Barnabas the right hand of fellowship, that we should go to the Gentiles and they to the circumcised; [10] only they would have us remember the poor, which very thing I was eager to do.

1. Language

VOCABULARY—*Barnabas* was a member of the earliest Jerusalem

67

church and originally from Cyprus (Acts 4:36–37). He had introduced Paul to the Jerusalem apostles (Acts 9:27), and later led the church at Antioch. He spearheaded with Paul the first missionary journey (Acts 13:1–3). Barnabas was an ideal companion to go with Paul to meet the other apostles because of his previous relationship to Jerusalem.

Titus was a Gentile convert of Paul's (2:3) who shared in his later ministry (See 2 Cor. 2:12–13, 7:6ff, 8:6ff, 8:16ff). The *uncircumcised* are the Gentiles who do not have the sign of the Covenant cut into the male reproductive organ. The *circumcised* are the Jews who have submitted to that rite (see Genesis 17:9–14) as a sign of belonging to God and keeping the Old Testament law. *Peter* and *Cephas* are used interchangeably for the premier apostle. *James,* as already noted, is the Lord's brother. *John* is one of the sons of Zebedee and from the original twelve (see Mark 1:19).

STYLE—Polemic history. The *then* in 2:1 connects structurally to the *then* in 1:18 and 1:21. Note also the time and place references. The fourteen years may refer to the time lapse between Paul's conversion or his first Jerusalem visit. Paul records encounters, conversations, and results in some detail, apparently answering key objections to his authority from this Jerusalem visit. The style is difficult at times, leaving, for example, a broken sentence in 2:4–5 as Paul's mind moves more quickly than his grammar over the points to be made. The theme again is the *gospel* (2:1, 5, 7).

2. **Historical**—Paul now deals with his second Jerusalem visit which is obviously crucial for him and his argument. Here he is confronted by the issue of circumcision. He not only holds fast to his understanding of the gospel, but is supported and affirmed by the pillar apostles. The result of this is a division of labor based on a unity of theology and sealed "in the right hand of fellowship" (2:9).

Paul begins his narration by identifying his companions, Barnabas, a Jewish member of the Jerusalem church, and Titus, a Gentile convert who demonstrates the validity of Paul's mission. Barnabas will be a trusted witness for Paul's case to those in authority, and Titus will be exhibit "A".

The Apostle goes to Jerusalem not summoned by those over him, but by the Lord himself, "by revelation" (2:2). There, however, in private discussion with the church leaders, Paul presents his gospel, the substance of the revelation given to him by Christ (1:12) and preached among the Gentiles (1:16). Titus, uncircumcised, is welcomed "as is" over the objections of "false brethren" who were smuggled into the private gathering (from Paul's point of view) and who sought to "lay down the law" to Paul and Titus, apparently demanding that the latter be circumcised. Paul, however, stands firm, and the leadership of the Jerusalem church accepted him and his position.

The evidence for their acceptance was Paul's grasp of the gospel (2:5, 7) which had been given to him by Christ, the witness of Titus and Barnabas to the results of his ministry, and as Paul says, "the grace that was given to me." This was enough for James, Cephas, and John. They extended their fellowship to Paul and Barnabas to evangelize the Gentiles as they did the Jews. Their only request was that Paul remember the poor, but he was already eager to do that (2:10).

To summarize: Paul goes to Jerusalem and meets privately with the church leaders. In the course of their conversations legalists demand Gentile circumcision, precipitating a crisis. Paul holds firm to the truth of his gospel and the evidence of his ministry which is then accepted by the Jerusalem leaders. In principle they are united. In practice they divide their ministry between Jew and Gentile. It is the principle, however, which is the heart of Paul's defense against his opponents in Galatia.

3. Theological—Paul sees his conference in Jerusalem as defending "the truth of the gospel" (2:5). This is, first, a theological reality (yet to be exposited in Galatians) relating to "our freedom which we have in Christ Jesus" (2:4), and also, second, a practical reality which means no circumcision of Gentile converts. Both principle and practice are accepted.

While Paul is confident of his apostleship and gospel, having received both by revelation, nevertheless he knows that his mission and message are a part of a larger whole centering historically in what Jesus Christ has done. Therefore Paul is both independent and interdependent. He can go so far as to say that he went to Jerusalem "lest somehow I should be running or had run in vain" (2:2). If he were rejected by the original apostles, how could he escape the conclusion that he was satanically deceived or self-deluded?

Thus two important points emerge from this passage: first, there must be a unity between our message and our life-style, and second, while we are independent in faith before God, we are also accountable to each other.

One further point may be mentioned: the importance of a division of labor. Some are better suited to reach Jews, others to reach Gentiles.

This strategic separation in the early church is not a sign of disunity but of wisdom. God gives varieties of gifts, personalities, and abilities. The early Christians realized this, tested Paul's message and results, then opened the door wide for his special role. Our unity in the gospel will allow infinite diversity in the way it is communicated to the world.

4. Strategic—Paul has given his final and crucial argument against his opponents. Not only has he received his apostleship and message directly from Christ, but this has been affirmed by the original apostles. The case against Paul can only be made by the legalists if they can prove that he misrepresents the intention of Jesus and those who shared in his earthly ministry. But the contrary is true.

Paul's visit to Jerusalem meant that although he was attacked by "false brethren" (2:4), as are the Galatians, he stood against them, the other apostles affirming his position. Thus, if Peter, James, and John were in Galatia, they would stand with Paul.

The only division in Jerusalem which resulted was a division of labor. This was made possible by the agreement that the apostles shared about the substance of the faith. Thus the independence of Paul in Galatians 1 is balanced by the interdependence of all the apostles in chapter 2. The church stands united against those who would pervert the faith in its highest leadership.

Opposition is there, to be sure. But these are "false brethren," who spy on Paul's freedom only to land him in bondage. As he did not yield to them then, so the Galatians must not yield to them now.

5. Contemporary—Paul demonstrates in this passage the necessity for a union between his message and his life-style. If he preaches freedom, then Titus must be left uncircumcised. The gospel cannot become mythological, unrelated to time and space. It is not some vague idealism, but a here and now demonstration of practical reality.

If we preach oneness in Christ, then our churches must not remain divided. If we preach God's free forgiveness, then we must open hands and hearts to those who hate our guts. If we denounce materialism, then we must not do it from the pulpit of our million-dollar sanctuary. If we claim Christ makes us brothers, then we must exhibit this in integrated fellowships.

Paul also demonstrates in this passage our independence and interdependence. Personal faith is demanded of each of us as it was of Paul. Christianity is no heirloom to be passed on from attic to attic. We must decide for or against Christ. We are personally responsible for our own "yes" or "no." At the same time, when Jesus Christ calls us to himself, he calls us to each other simultaneously. We are now accountable to a body of believers who are fellow adventurers in Christ. They will love us, accept us, and, when necessary, correct us. Christianity is personal but not individualistic and even Paul with his overwhelming sense of authority witnesses to this as he goes off to Jerusalem. Christians cut off from the mainstream of historic faith and theology become unbalanced freaks. In the right hand of fellowship someone else holds us as the sign of our belonging to each other.

At the same time, the division of labor means that we must accept each others' uniqueness. Paul goes to the Gentiles; Peter to the Jews. Evangelism is stifled when we demand that everyone do it our way. A man converted by reading a tract will probably pass out many more, but we do not all have to pass tracts. God has different people, different methods, different ministries—bound together by the same message. This the apostles discovered in Jerusalem. How long will it take for our rediscovery?

6. **Personal**—Paul made his case in Jerusalem using Barnabas the bridge builder and Titus the indisputable example. These brothers incarnated the reality which Paul shared, demonstrating the grace given to him (2:9). Out of this sharing came a wider fellowship with Peter, James, and John.

I do not have to go it alone. There is a Barnabas, a reconciler to stand with me. There is a Titus, a demonstrator, to go with me. And out of that fellowship an even larger one will emerge.

When we opened the Salt Company Coffee House in Hollywood in 1968 there was a body around me to enter into ministry. John Block, a professional basketball player, was our construction superintendent. Doug Oliver, an electrician, built our sound system. Lance Bowen, an artist, designed the interior. Bob Marlowe, Brian Hahn, Pam VanValin, and David Covington formed a musical group. The Body of Christ flowed together to do a job, and out of this grew a much wider fellowship. A crucial test for my future ministry is this: Is there a growing, gifted body coming together to share the vision and the work? If not we must not go to our Jerusalem. God's time is not ours.

Galatians
2:11–21

11 But when Cephas came to Antioch I opposed him to his face, because he stood condemned. ¹² For before certain men came from James, he ate with the Gentiles; but when they came he drew back and separated himself, fearing the circumcision party. ¹³ And with him the rest of the Jews acted insincerely, so that even Barnabas was carried away by their insincerity. ¹⁴ But when I saw that they were not straightforward about the truth of the gospel, I said to Cephas before them all, "If you, though a Jew, live like a Gentile and not like a Jew, how can you compel the Gentiles to live like Jews?" ¹⁵ We ourselves, who are Jews by birth and not Gentile sinners, ¹⁶ yet who know that a man is not justified by works of the law but through faith in Jesus Christ, even we have believed in Christ Jesus, in order to be justified by faith in Christ, and not by works of the law, because by works of the law shall no one be justified. ¹⁷ But if, in our endeavor to be justified in Christ, we ourselves were found to be sinners, is Christ then an agent of sin? Certainly not! ¹⁸ But if I build up again those things which I tore down, then I prove myself a transgressor. ¹⁹ For I through the law died to the law, that I might live to God. ²⁰ I have been crucified with Christ; it is no longer I who live, but Christ who lives in me; and the life I now live in the flesh I live by faith in the Son of God, who loved me and gave himself for me. ²¹ I do not nullify the grace of God; for if justification were through the law, then Christ died to no purpose.

1. Language

VOCABULARY—*Antioch* was the capital of Syria, one of the three greatest cities of the Roman Empire and an early center of Christianity (Acts 11:19). Barnabas and Paul were both leaders in the church there (Acts 13:1–2). *Justified:* a legal term expressing the sentence of "not guilty" in a court of law. Usually, in Pauline thought, to be justified means to be accepted as not guilty before God. *Law:* the Old Testament moral and ritual code. *Faith:* a personal willful act of surrender to Jesus Christ issuing in salvation.

STYLE—From historical account—names, places, conversation—to theological exposition. Cephas is the prime figure again as in 1:18 and 2:1–10.

Here for the first time, after establishing a secure historical base in chapters 1 and 2, Paul begins to deal directly with theological issues. From 2:15 on, *justified* is used five times, *law* six times and *faith* three times. The section from 2:15–21 contains difficult and close theological reasoning and is filled with prepositional phrases expressing the difference between law and faith. Notice also that Paul becomes personal starting in 2:18, using *I*. Theology becomes the source of experience as it leads to the one who is life itself.

2. Historical—If the issue in Jerusalem is theology, the issue in Antioch is practice. Here the "truth of the gospel" (2:14, see 2:5) is defended by Paul against Peter's hypocrisy.

Peter has come to Antioch and eaten with the Gentiles violating Jewish dietary laws. He has acted consistently with the position reached in Jerusalem. However, when "certain men came from James" (2:12), Peter withdrew, "fearing the circumcision party." All of the Jews including Barnabas followed suit until Paul walked in. Incensed, he lectured Peter, and this rejoinder transitions into the first major theological exposition of the letter.

Who the "certain men from James" and the "circumcision party" are, we do not know. If they fully represented James' position, it is hard to understand his role in the decision in Jerusalem, giving Paul the right hand of fellowship over against the discredited "false brethren." At the same time, they undoubtedly represented part of James' conservatism concerning the Jewish law. They probably, however, carried it to an extreme as over-zealous disciples are apt to do. Whether these are the same opponents who later surfaced in Galatia we do not know. Certainly legalism was a problem for the whole church both theologically and practically, and this letter represents only one battle fought repeatedly in Paul's life and in every generation of Christians. That the opponents in Galatia had some relation to Jerusalem is evident from the charges Paul is answering in chapters 1 and 2 concerning his relationship with Peter and the Jerusalem church.

3. Theological—Paul sees that the "truth of the gospel" (2:14) must be defended in both theology and practice; he demands a wholeness to the Christian life.

His rejoinder to Peter starting in 2:14 leads us into the first strictly theological section. Paul's argument begins with Peter's behavior—you live like a Gentile, eating with everybody—now, under pressure, you are forcing the Gentiles to separate from you by separating from them. This then leads the Apostle into his theological discourse.

Paul's major points are as follows:

1. Even we Jews have believed in Christ to receive God's justification, his "not guilty" by faith.

2. We have done this because we accept the axiom "by works of the law shall *no one* be justified" (2:16). This includes even we Jews who have tried to live a moral life to earn God's acceptance.

3. Since we have admitted that we are sinners does that mean that Christ is the cause of our sin? No! But if we drag back in the law, then we will arouse the sinful rebellion to which we have died through the law.

4. My experience verifies this theology. The law showed me my sin. It drove me in helplessness to Christ. I identified with Christ in his death on the cross, where he took the legal demand and penalty for sin upon himself, thus I died there too by faith when I gave up trying to be good and accepted Christ's goodness as my own.

5. Now I am alive to God. My old self-righteous, legal self is dead at the cross. I no longer live an egotistical, self-centered life, but Christ lives in me in his resurrection life.

6. This new life is still "in the flesh," the real me, but it is lived not by legal performance, but by faith, secured in the love of the Son of God.

7. Thus, if I bring back in the law to work my way to God, Christ had no reason to die.

The difficulties in unraveling all of this lie, in part, in the technical language, and, in part, in the lack of explanation and illustration. Paul condenses his conclusions, probably summarizing his response to Peter. He anticipates himself here and will give a more comprehensive elaboration in chapters 3 and 4. This, however, in brief, is his reply to the legalists in Antioch and Galatia.

Even the Jews admit that they cannot work their way to God. They have placed their faith in Christ, surrendering their legal righteousness in frustration. The reason for this is that "by works of the law shall no one be justified" (2:16). Paul simply states this, offering no reasons. They lie, however, in the frailty of human nature—we sinners lack the power to keep the law—and in the inadequacy of the law itself: it is impressed upon us from the outside and has no power to secure its own enforcement.

Paul rejects the assertion that Christ is the agent of sin with a "Certainly not!" (2:17), since he has revealed the inability of the Jews to keep the law. In other words, Paul does not pause to debate the point. Christ, of course, is not the agent of sin since he only shows the inability of the sinner to fulfill the law's demand. In fact, Christ is the agent of righteousness since he not only fulfills the law's demand in his holy life and takes the law's punishment upon himself in his death, but, most important, he now gives us the power to live a holy life through his Spirit "by faith."

To reintroduce the law, "to build up again the things which I tore down" is to really become a transgressor, because once the law comes in again the problem of my rebellion and the law's impotence to empower its own fulfillment is reintroduced.

The law, by convicting me of sin and exposing my impotence, leads me to despair and in that I am ready to accept Christ's death on my behalf. When I do that I die to the law, the old legal demands (2:19), and find a new life with God. This Paul expresses in the classic verse in 2:20 where he recounts his identification with the death of Christ. In despair I cast myself on Christ, and his death fulfilling the law becomes my death, cancelling the law's claim on me. As Bill Counts says, "We do not meet Christ at the cross, we meet him *on* the cross." In this death to the independent, self-righteous, self-asserting self, life now comes. "Christ lives in me." Once sin is done in, Christ can now reside in my body, the moral dilemma of my being a sinner and God being holy is resolved. Now life is lived in constant trust in the Christ who verified himself as trustworthy in his self-giving love. The heart of Paul's theology, this gospel revealed to the Apostle and defended and accepted in Jerusalem, will become clearer as we study the great middle section of the letter.

4. Strategic—Paul's final response to the legalists is to recount his stand against Peter's hypocrisy in Antioch. Although the Jewish Christians separated from the Gentile Christians under the pressure of the "circumcision party," and although even Barnabas, as Paul admits, joined them, all was suspended when Paul called the whole lot on their insincerity.

Thus, while this event may seem to be ammunition for Paul's opponents, in fact it is not. If the division still existed in Antioch, Paul would have not dared to bring this up. However, he shows that while he and Peter agreed in principle in Jerusalem (2:1–10), that still had to be worked out in practice. Peter's insincerity is seen in his ambivalent behavior before and after the "circumcision party" arrived. Paul would not stand for it. He had sound theological reasons, which he proceeds to relate. Thus Peter's theological agreement in Jerusalem and eating with Gentiles in Antioch (2:12) support Paul's position. His shift under pressure is attacked by the Apostle, but this final incident still supports the essential unity of Paul and Peter, not only in theology but behavior. Since Paul saw through to the heart of the issue which was salvation itself, and no mere compromise on the custom of eating together, he alone stood and called the rest back to the truth of the gospel (2:14). So he also does with the Galatians.

5. **Contemporary**—"Don't rock the boat." "These things take time." How often we hear that in the church and the world. "If we do that we will offend our old members, and remember, they support the church." Paul will have nothing of this when principle is at stake. If Jews and Gentiles do not eat together, how can we tell the world that reconciliation has been accomplished? The gospel again becomes mythology.

Christianity is exciting when it cannot be explained away psychologically and sociologically. Even the casual observer can figure out why church people are together. They share a common racial background; they live in a certain part of town; they are socially compatible. There is often nothing going on here any more unique than at the local Rotary Club.

When the expected patterns are broken, however, questions are raised and not so easily answered. How can Jews and Gentiles eat together and live together? What has happened to overturn thousands of years of exclusivism and hostility? This demonstration of the reality is what Paul is fighting for. If the gospel is not happening in our relationships, it is not happening at all.

In the summer of 1970 we opened a house on Virgil Street in Los Angeles for "crashers." In that first summer we had living with us a seminary student, several college students, an ex-homosexual drag queen from Hollywood, a black from Philadelphia, ex-drug addicts, and a twenty-nine-year-old from Tennessee who could neither read nor write and who had built a cabin in Yosemite. Here we were, under one roof, facing the question, what do these people have in common? What holds them together? There was but one answer: Jesus Christ, and in that demonstration there was more real evangelism going on than I had ever seen.

The world is waiting for our evidence that Christ has made us one. Seeing is believing when we sit down to eat together.

6. Personal—Bonhoeffer writes, "When Jesus calls a man he bids him come and die." Paul tells us that he has been crucified with Christ. There is nothing more final than death, and I naturally recoil from it.

I want life, I want resurrection, but on my terms, not God's. God's way is the way of the cross. Only in death to my securities, to my self-centered life, to my sin, can I find Christ's life in me.

How I want to hang on. I grasp my wife, my paycheck, my institutional position, my intellectual accomplishment, my health, my friends. They will justify my life. They will guarantee its meaning. They will fulfill me. But satisfaction eludes me because God has made me for more. At last, reduced again to emptiness, I face the cross. Jesus dies there abandoning all. Alluring me with his love, staggering me with the awe-full cost, I come to join him. My collection of honors, recognition, things, even people, fall through my fingers like sand. As Luther says, I give up the bright light of reason for the darkness of faith. There, at the cross, in darkness, Christ's death is my death and the miracle happens. When I open my hand to Christ, letting go of my toys which I have grasped with such seriousness, he not only takes my hand, but fills it with himself. "It is no longer I who live, but Christ who lives in me." In my darkness, a new light dawns, the light of faith, the light of Jesus' presence. My spirit soars; life floods in. Now I live. "I live by faith in the Son of God, who loved *me* and gave himself for *me*." At last I can speak, not merely of the world, of the church, or even of "us" but of "me." Christ is mine and I am his, forever.

Questions for Discussion and Reflection: Chapter 2

2:1–10

1. Where is my faith supported by another brother or sister?
2. Where is my faith demonstrated in a principle I cannot surrender or in a life that is bound to me?
3. How well do I accept the diversity in Christ's body? How free am I from the demand that all be like me?
4. Think of the Christian group which most bothers me. Why do I

become upset? What strengths do they reveal? What points do I share in common with them? How can I discover unity in Christ with them?

5. What divides Christians—message or methods? If methods, how can that be overcome?

6. Focus in on one brother who uses different methods of ministry. How can I give him the "right hand of fellowship" this week?

2:11–21

7. How is the truth of the gospel demonstrated in my behavior? If the test of my Christianity is "observed behavioral changes," how do I pass the test?

8. If today I ceased to be a Christian, how would that immediately change my behavior?

9. How personal is my faith? Do I feel the "who loved me" in Paul?

10. What does "meeting Jesus on the cross" mean in my life? What major things must I die to?

3
Galatians
3:1-5

3 O foolish Galatians! Who has bewitched you, before whose eyes Jesus Christ was publicly portrayed as crucified? ² Let me ask you only this: Did you receive the Spirit by works of the law, or by hearing with faith? ³ Are you so foolish? Having begun with the Spirit, are you now ending with the flesh? ⁴ Did you experience so many things in vain?—if it really is in vain. ⁵ Does he who supplies the Spirit to you and works miracles among you do so by works of the law, or by hearing with faith?

1. Language

VOCABULARY—*The Spirit:* the Holy Spirit, God's imminent presence with and in us which unites us to Christ. *The flesh:* life lived simply on human strength, without the power and presence of God. Therefore, the flesh designates a selfish, futile and transitory life. *Miracles:* direct actions of God which speed up or suspend natural processes of cause and effect.

STYLE—Intensely polemic and argumentative. Paul turns on his readers with exclamations and rhetorical questions. His words are emotional and biting: "foolish," "bewitched," "in vain."

2. Historical—

Paul returns again to the experience of the Galatians. Jesus Christ was preached publicly to them as crucified (3:1). They heard the message and responded with faith (3:5). The result of this was the entrance of the Spirit into them (3:2, 3, 5) and the verification of his presence through miraculous signs (3:5). Thus Paul recalls the

79

Galatians' conversion and in so doing shows us his basic evangelistic procedure. Now, however, the churches have come under a spell. They are "bewitched" (3:1). They are "foolish," for they are abandoning the reality of their early experience and surrendering the very means of life, "ending in the flesh" (3:3). If they do this, all that has happened to them is in vain (3:4).

3. Theological—Paul helps us in understanding the reception and function of the Spirit. The vital means of the Christian life is now introduced for the first time.

The Spirit comes in the context of evangelical preaching: Jesus Christ as crucified. It is this message, this word of God, which is the vehicle of the Spirit's revelation and illumination. The power of the Spirit is released when the truth of the gospel is announced. It is this gospel which he has promised to bless, and through which he operates on the human heart.

The message must be proclaimed in the world, publicly (3:1), to non-believers. When it is heralded the Spirit is supplied as the listeners hear and respond not "by works of the law," but "by hearing with faith" (3:2). Thus, Paul excludes all steps to receiving the Holy Spirit except hearing and believing in the gospel. This includes, of course, for Paul repentance and confession of sin, but all of this is a part of the response of faith. The Apostle does not offer several steps to the Holy Spirit: watching, fasting, praying, waiting, etc. When a person hears the gospel and receives Jesus Christ, its subject, the Spirit enters his life.

Thus, the Christian life is "begun in the Spirit" (3:3). There is no possibility of being a Christian and later receiving the Holy Spirit. The Spirit is the author of new life in Christ. The Spirit now continues to be the operative power of the Christian life, the source of Christian experience, the worker of miracles (3:4–5).

All rules and regulations for receiving the Spirit or living in the fullness of the Spirit must be abandoned. This would be re-introducing the "works of the law" (3:2, 5). The Spirit begins and continues his operation in us "by faith." Thus we cannot manipulate him or force his hand even by pious activity. This would all be "ending in the flesh," trying to get God to bless us or gift us, probably for our own selfishness, even the selfishness of a "truly" spiritual existence.

The Christian life is begun by faith in Christ and it is sustained by the same saving faith. Through this faith, the Spirit works from beginning to end. It is just that simple.

4. Strategic—After a lengthy historical and theological exposition, Paul calls his hearers to attention: "O foolish Galatians!" This is similar in tactics to 1:6, "I am astonished." Just in case they were lost in his theology, or their minds had begun to wander, the Apostle restores them with a new blast.

Again, Paul appeals to their experience before launching into his major theological exposition. Thus he is not merely gaining their attention, but also forcing them to face the existential relevance of what he is about to say. They cannot dispute their own experience.

Paul's charge is biting: they are "bewitched," they are under a spell. Only in this way can he explain their desertion of the gospel, their cutting themselves off from the Spirit, and their return to "the flesh" (3:3).

Once again, to use a military metaphor, Paul blasts a hole in the Galatians' defense by this harsh attack, and then rushes sound theological argument through the breach before they can recover (3:6ff). It is an overwhelming confrontation.

5. Contemporary—There is great confusion in the church today over the Holy Spirit. This is ironic because the Spirit is often described as the Spirit of unity in the Bible. At the same time, this confusion is understandable because major theologians have been largely silent on the doctrine of the Holy Spirit, the institutional church has often quenched the Spirit, and the Biblical teaching on the Spirit is at times unsystematic.

Thus, we see in Pentecostalism a new grasp of the centrality of the Spirit which is touching all major Christian denominations. While this openness to the Spirit is perhaps the great event in the church today, the danger of a new legalism entering in concerning the Spirit is apparent. For this reason, Paul's words in 3:1–5 are timely and essential.

Paul connects the Spirit fundamentally to evangelism. Rather than praying for more of the Spirit or the power of the Spirit, we need preach the gospel, so that the Spirit can be manifest through the means which he has chosen, the word of the cross.

Paul also connects the Spirit fundamentally to faith. If the Christian life is begun by faith it is sustained by faith. There is nothing more necessary to receive God's blessing than the simple faith exercised in conversion. At the same time, the Spirit continues to operate in our lives with many experiences and miracles (3:3, 5). Thus we can expect signs of the Spirit as our Christian lives grow. But what is the source? The same faith which we exercised when we first believed.

One reason why so many are abandoning the church today is because of its lack of spiritual power. It is held to be a social club, or a fortress, or a place for religious people, but it is not seen as a center of spiritual life. Bazaars, picnics, church league basketball, ski trips, and hay rides may be means of the Spirit, but they are not the signs of the Holy Spirit. As Vern Bullock says, "Before I became a Christian I thought the church was a sterile, stuffy, stale place. After I became a Christian, I knew the church was a sterile, stuffy, stale place."

But where Christians gather to celebrate the gospel, where the Spirit is free to change lives, where miracles begin to occur, the church comes alive.

6. **Personal**—Am I ending with the flesh? It is a constant struggle not to do so. How easily I project a performance-oriented culture into my Christian life. If I pray more, if I am more bold in my witness, if I study the Bible more, if I attend church, then God will bless me. So I work on one area of my spiritual life, only to let another sag. I pour time into prayer and study to develop my interior spiritual life and neglect my friends and the needy around me. Or I jump into society to prove the relevancy of my faith and neglect its source.

I have often felt defeated in my Christian life. I remember seeking power from God, praying for power, attending prayer meetings where power was promised. Then it struck me, when Christ is preached as crucified, the power is released. Perhaps if I shared Christ more I would need more power, not for my spiritual flights, but for God's glory. When in weakness and fear and trembling, I have shared my faith, the Spirit's power has accompanied me. The miracles have been seen.

Galatians
3:6–9

6 Thus Abraham "believed God, and it was reckoned to him as righteousness." 7 So you see that it is men of faith who are the sons of Abraham. 8 And the scripture, foreseeing that God would justify the Gentiles by faith, preached the gospel beforehand to Abraham, saying, "In you shall all the nations be blessed." 9 So then, those who are men of faith are blessed with Abraham who had faith.

1. Language

VOCABULARY—*Abraham:* the father of the Jewish race and the prototype of the man of faith (Genesis 12:1ff). *Reckoned:* accounted, regarded as. *Righteousness:* moral perfection before a holy God, in right standing before God.

STYLE—highly theological: thesis, argument, and conclusion. Paul's use of the Old Testament is particularly effective in refuting his legalistic opponents. The word *faith* appears four times and is thematic.

2. Historical—There is nothing here which illumines Paul, the Galatians, or their opponents, except that the argument based on Abraham would impress those tempted to go under the Old Testament law.

3. Theological—Paul argues for the priority of faith, founding his thesis on Abraham. In the life of the father of the Jewish race, in the prototype of all believers, the gospel has been demonstrated. First, Abraham believed God. Second, he received from God the gift of rightstanding before him. Third, he heard the good news that all the nations would be blessed, that is, receive salvation, through him.

Paul immediately quotes from Genesis 15:6 which establishes Abraham's faith and righteousness. This is the test of true spiritual experience—God's acceptance is received "by faith." Based on faith, God pronounced, *reckoned,* Abraham righteous. His standing before God had nothing to do with accomplishment; it had everything to do with taking God at his word.

Paul now applies this truth: "So you see that it is men of faith who are the sons of Abraham" (3:7). For the Apostle the true son reflects the character of his father. Since Abraham had faith, the Galatians will be his sons, not because of the Jewish blood in their veins or the sign of the covenant cut in their flesh, but because they share Abraham's character, namely, faith (3:7).

To *faith* and *righteousness* Paul adds the *blessing.* God's acceptance of Abraham was not for him alone. He looked down the generations to the nations and promised his blessing, his salvation, to all by faith. Thus Abraham heard the gospel, the good news, which we have received, in his promise (3:8).

Father Abraham is no isolated figure. He inaugurated the gospel and by his example guarantees that the Galatians' spiritual experience (3:1–5) and ours is true, rooted in the faithfulness of God.

The theological importance of this for Paul is:

1. It grounds the gospel in the Old Testament. God has consistently revealed himself as giving the blessing to those who believe him. Paul's message is no surprise, no deviation from the Old Testament revelation.

2. Righteousness is God's gift to those who believe him. Thus, circumcision and legal obedience are at best signs of faith, and unnecessary to the man, who like Abraham, has faith.

3. Paul's mission to the Gentiles is based in God's promise to Abraham. The Apostle to the Gentiles plays a crucial role in God's purpose to fulfill his promise.

4. **Strategic**—Paul pulls a coup on the Jew by jumping over Moses and going back to Abraham, who started everything. For the Jew it was "Moses, Moses, Moses." Moses was the great deliverer who brought Israel out of Egypt. Moses was the great law-giver who brought God's moral will to the people. The rabbis ultimately traced all of their teaching back to Moses. Judaism in the first century was "Torah-centric": centered in the law of God.

Once, however, Paul came to Christ, he saw that behind Moses stood Abraham, the father of the Jewish race. Long before the law was given, before there was legal righteousness by performance, Abraham trusted God and was reckoned, accepted as righteous.

Thus Paul's tactic is dramatic and telling. Leaping over Moses, he presents Abraham, the first Jew, as a man of faith. Thus, if the Galatians who are in danger of going under the law want to be true Jews, they must be like Abraham—sharing his faith.

To defend his argument, Paul quotes from the Old Testament. This again, is a damaging point against the legalists who claim to uphold the scriptures. Abraham was reckoned righteous by faith in Genesis 15:6, and God promised to bless all nations through Abraham in Genesis 12:3. If the legalists are to make their case for accepting the Jewish law they must avoid father Abraham and deny the foundational scriptures from Genesis.

5. **Contemporary**—We are a rootless generation. The disasters morally and politically of the 20th century have cut us loose from history. The post-World War II despair was summed up by a scrawl on a French café, "Don't kill time, kill yourself." Yet, from the further dislocations of the later 60s and 70s, there has come a nostalgia for the

past. Antique collecting, leaving the city for a simpler life, and country and western music have all affected us.

In this quest for roots, Paul offers a heritage which goes back almost 4,000 years: sons of Abraham by faith.

The question of identity plagues us all. "Who am I?" we ask. "Where can I find stability, some permanent focus for my life?" Once again Paul offers a belonging centered in God's acceptance of Abraham.

I remember attending a Roman Catholic wedding where the Mass was said in Latin. There the thought struck me: this same service was going on a thousand years ago, and the chills ran up my spine. In a greater way, when we share Abraham's faith, we find that we belong to a history extending to the Fertile Crescent at the end of the Sumerian civilization. Our human identity is shared with the first man to take God at his word and adventure with him.

Today three major religions, Christian, Jewish, and Muslim honor Abraham. We can more than honor him, we can belong to him as we know his God and share his faith. Here are roots for a rootless time.

6. **Personal**—"Men of faith are blessed" (3:9). This is hard to believe, it is so intangible. Faith seems to be such a cop-out. Yet, if we were to change the verse to "men of vision are blessed," we might see it better.

Several years ago, my friend Bob Marlowe asked me if I wanted to hear some Dylan records. Being in the Ray Conniff era, I was not sure, but I went with him. After getting over the culture shock of Dylan's nasal singing, I began to hear his lyrics and in them were reflected the cries and longings of a generation.

Why couldn't I use this music to punctuate a sermon? With Bob playing Dylan on his guitar and my preaching the biblical answer to Dylan's questions, we ventured out. The response was overwhelming. Our evening services grew to over 1,200 in attendance. But we needed a place to do this communication regularly, where the unchurched would feel at home. An old apartment building became the first Salt Company Coffee House. This led to crash pads, a job corps, and a leadership training center. "Men of faith" are blessed. Where with little faith I have ventured out the blessing has been sure to come.

Galatians
3:10–14

10 For all who rely on works of the law are under a curse; for it is written, "Cursed be every one who does not abide by all things written in the book of the law, and do them." ¹¹ Now it is evident that no man is justified before God by the law; for "He who through faith is righteous shall live",¹² but the law does not rest on faith, for "He who does them shall live by them." ¹³ Christ redeemed us from the curse of the law, having become a curse for us—for it is written, "Cursed be every one who hangs on a tree"—¹⁴ that in Christ Jesus the blessing of Abraham might come upon the Gentiles, that we might receive the promise of the Spirit through faith.

1. Language

VOCABULARY—*Redeemed:* to be brought out of bondage, to be purchased from slavery, to be set free.

STYLE—The theological argument continues with each point justified from the Old Testament. Faith is a key word appearing in 3:12 and 3:14. At the same time *curse* appears four times posing the alternative to faith.

2. Historical—Again, nothing here illumines Paul, the Galatians, or the opponents except the thrust of the argument.

3. Theological—Paul has established that Abraham was accepted before God by faith and through him, the man of faith, salvation was promised to the nations. Now the Apostle is ready to deal with the law, with Moses.

In contrast to Abraham's faith and the promise of blessing, the law brings a curse upon us. The curse is in its total demand, that we abide by *all things* written in the book of the law and do them (3:10). There is no compromise; it is all or nothing. We are either law keepers or law breakers. The standard is absolute, God's holy character.

We have two alternatives. We may strive to be perfect by keeping the whole law (3:12), or we may surrender this idle dream and receive God's gift of righteousness by faith (3:11). It is our pride and arrogance which keeps us from accepting God's verdict, "He who through faith is righteous shall live" (3:11 and Habakkuk 2:4).

Now we have an apparent contradiction. On the one hand, in Abraham we have the promise of blessing, and on the other hand, in Moses we have the warning of the curse. God promises to accept us by faith, then loads us with the demand of keeping the whole law. He appears schizophrenic.

For Paul, while God does love us and asks us to trust him, he is still holy. The classic question, "How can a sinner stand in the presence of a holy God?" remains valid. Our sense of alienation is not merely natural, the result of our higher evolution, or existential, because of a meaningless universe. It is moral. We are guilty sinners, and God is absolute holiness, a consuming fire. But it is just at this point of the apparent contradiction between the promise and the curse that Christ is offered as the divine resolution.

Christ has come and taken the curse of the law, our moral failure and God's just judgment for it, upon himself. His holy life fulfills the demand of the law for perfection. His death, then, is not for his own sin, since he has none. It is voluntary, for us. Removing, then, the barrier of sin and its penalty of death in his cross, and granting us his forgiveness, now the blessing of Abraham is ours by faith.

In this sense, God resolves the problem of his own holiness and love in the death of Christ for sin. Removing the barrier himself, he welcomes us as sons of Abraham when we place our trust in him.

The substitutionary nature of Christ's death is enshrined in the phrase "having become a curse for us" (3:13). As James Denney remarks, "Christ did not just become a man, he became a curse." Love only becomes understandable when we see that it acts properly according to the circumstances. As Denney illustrates, if I were sitting on a dock and a man ran down the pier yelling, "I love you, I love you," and then jumped into the river and drowned, I would believe him crazy. But if I fell off the dock and was being carried away in the rapids and a man yelling "I love you" jumped in and rescued me, I would be forever grateful, believing his love.

So Christ jumped in, taking the curse which stands over us, and from our rescue comes eternal gratitude.

With the curse lifted, the promised blessing given to Abraham is now ours (3:14). The reality of this promise is verified in the presence of the Spirit, "through faith." Thus, Paul has given the theological foundation for his experiential argument in 3:1–5.

For Paul, heresy is Christ plus anything. The Galatians are in danger of falling for Christ plus the law, Christ plus circumcision, Christ plus good works. The Apostle shows the impossibility of this. It is either Christ or the law, the promise or the curse, faith or good works. Those who would add legalism to Christ ultimately destroy his work. Either he took the curse of the law or he did not. If he took it, then I cannot. I must simply thank him for it and surrender into his arms.

4. **Strategic**—Now Paul has the legalists where he wants them. The law is a curse because of its absolute nature. The law contradicts the Old Testament promise that "He who through faith is righteous shall live" (3:11). The law makes God schizophrenic. Paul shows from logic and Old Testament scripture then, the necessity of Christ; he has come to resolve the conflict. He takes the curse and gives the blessing, verified in the Spirit, and received by faith.

How can the legalists deny the priority of Abraham? How can they deny the totality of the law's claim? How can they deny the finality and completeness of Christ's work? Paul has shut them out on their own ground, the Old Testament revelation.

5. **Contemporary**—Legalism rears its ugly head in every generation. The church must continually guard the ramparts against the "curse of the law." In modern theology both conservatism and liberalism have, practically speaking, tended to end up under the curse. The conservatives have put their followers under the curse of a rigid moralism to express their separation from the world. The liberals have put their followers under the curse of a humanitarianism which has justified their faith as "relevant." Both sides have ended in not seeing the seriousness of the curse.

The curse comes in the demand for perfection. I want the highest and the best but cannot achieve it. The curse comes in anxiety as I strive to fulfill it. I fear failure. I try harder. Am I measuring up? The curse comes in the exhaustion of performance, I am strung out on my own effort. Finally, the curse comes either by the prideful illusion of accomplishment or the guilt produced by failure. Either way the results reinforce my selfishness and thus reveal my sin.

The "curse of the law" needs to be revealed to a legalistic, competitive church. Gold stars for memory verses, attendance badges, honor rolls, recognition for financial support—all bear the curse of the law. The system of the church often teaches me that I am accepted because I am a good performer. For the morally sensitive, this becomes the curse of the law. For all, this stands as a barrier to accepting the sheer and complete grace of Christ.

The "curse of the law" needs to be revealed to a legalistic, competitive society. Ashley Montague, the founder of the sociology department at Rutgers University says that the American home is the most dehumanizing institution in the world, because it teaches performance for acceptance. Here is conditional love—"I love you, but." Our children are socialized into good performers, to achieve in the educational, social, and economic systems. This achievement then proves their value to society, their families and themselves. The "curse of the law" stands as a witness to the stupidity of this motive for performance. Our life-style is merely a coverup for the jungle of lust, pride, and egotism within. Again, the curse is the absolute demand of a holy God which cannot ultimately be met by our achievements or rationalized by the dulling of our conscience. The painful diagnosis of a doctor is welcome if it leads to healing. Therefore, let us welcome the "curse of the law" which brings us to Christ.

6. **Personal**—When I entered college as a new Christian I was 3,000 miles from home, friendless, and extremely insecure. I was invited to a Bible study led by a vigorous group of Christians who would welcome me if I carried a King James Bible, witnessed door-to-door in the dorms and did not attend dances or movies.

Because I needed their friendship I readily agreed to the terms. I spent many evenings calling on my classmates, warning them of hell. I was a model Christian by the group's standards (except that I secretly continued to attend movies, much to my inner shame).

After the year ended I boarded a flight home and sat beside an oriental woman on her way to Hawaii. My first thought was "I must witness to her." My second thought was "I don't want to witness to her." Then I realized the reason, I had no member of the group around to boast to of my accomplishment. I flew home in despair.

I have known the curse of performance, and I have known the intense curse of God's holiness. Thus, I celebrate the gospel. "Christ redeemed us from the curse of the law . . ." (3:13). To know that my burden is gone, to know that I am loved and accepted as I am in Christ; to know that I do not have to perform any more; to know that I am free in God's forgiveness and love, is to know that beyond the curse is the blessing and that today Christ's hands are still open only to bless.

Galatians
3:15–18

15 To give a human example, brethren: no one annuls even a man's will, or adds to it, once it has been ratified. ¹⁶ Now the promises were made to Abraham and to his offspring. It does not say, "And to offsprings," referring to many; but, referring to one, "And to your offspring," which is Christ. ¹⁷ This is what I mean: the law, which came four hundred and thirty years afterward, does not annul a covenant previously ratified by God, so as to make the promise void. ¹⁸ For if the inheritance is by the law, it is no longer by promise; but God gave it to Abraham by a promise.

1. Language

VOCABULARY—*Covenant:* an agreement initiated by God, accepted by man which is a guarantee of their relationship.

STYLE—At last, Paul pauses for an illustration, "To give a human example, brethren" (3:15), as he continues to justify his argument from the Old Testament.

2. Historical—Again we have no immediate help in understanding Paul, the Galatians, or their opponents.

3. Theological—Paul has stated that the promise in Abraham and the curse in the law are resolved in Christ. He now stops to illustrate the compact theology in 3:6–14.

In human experience when a will has been made by a man, it cannot be changed. Thus the promise of blessing made to Abraham by God must stand regardless of what came later. This promise was made to Abraham and his "offspring" which Paul takes as a prophecy of Christ.

The law of Moses came four hundred and thirty years later (3:17). Thus it cannot modify or change God's previous promise, since he offered the inheritance (as in a human will) freely, and the demand of the law has not altered that. God did not make one plan and then change his mind and make another. He is consistent and faithful to his covenant promise.

Paul also implies here the inferiority of the law chronologically. It came much later than the promise. The promise is the foundation upon which all else was built.

4. Strategic—Paul knows that he has not fully satisfied the legalists in 3:6–14. They will reply that the law of God has superseded the promise to Abraham. "God saved the best until last." They will ask, "Why did God lay the law on us if he did not plan for us to fulfill it?" They will object that Paul's message opens the door to moral degeneration and presumption if we no longer have to keep the law.

So now Paul pauses for illustration and elaboration. If God is consistent in his character, if his word is true, if his promise is faithful, then what he said to Abraham must come to pass. Ultimately, it is the character of God which is at stake. Thus, whatever the law does, it cannot contradict God's character. This is the unresolved tension in Judaism. God's holiness and love, law and grace; particularism and universalism.

5. Contemporary—The world asks, will God be faithful to his promise although the evidence seems to go against it? A hotel fire takes the lives of nine children. An earthquake shatters a city in the Andes. Death reduces a family to poverty. Cancer eats up a human body. Where, before the evidence of sorrow, grief, and suffering is the promise of God's love?

Sensitive men have cried out in the darkness throughout history, if not for love, then for justice. And we must admit, God at times keeps his silence or as here, appears to contradict himself.

So in desperation, like the legalists, we struggle for alternatives. Perhaps I have to do it myself. If God will not speak, I will. My philosophy will justify my life. My morality will provide a way. My enlightenment will put humanity on the path to suffering's end.

But faith demands trust even against the evidence. This is, in Kierkegaard's terms, the "passion of faith." God will be true to his promise. All the evidence is not in yet. Then suddenly the morning star rises. The sky is filled with angels. God breaks his silence. And we have learned the futility of our small solutions, and patience and trust even when the evidence is to the contrary. In Jesus Christ God comes to share the agony of our life and to seal in his blood his own participation both in the human dilemma and its resolution.

6. Personal—How do I deal with "contradictions" in the Bible? God seems to save me by promise and then by performance.

I have learned over the years that often the contradictions are in my head. The problem may be the way I ask the questions or my shallow grasp of the evidence. Someone defined Christianity as "faith working toward understanding."

The issue is, do I trust the character of God? Will his covenant stand? If so, then I can relax. I can afford to work on the problems and still praise God. I discover that the easiest thing to change is my mind. My mental state must not determine my faith.

So the promise to Abraham and the law of Moses seem to contradict each other. I must be failing to understand them. At this point I am ready and open for a new perspective, and in Christ I know God's intention to resolve the ambiguities and finally to shatter the glass darkly, that I may see him face to face.

Galatians
3:19–20

19 Why then the law? It was added because of transgressions, till the offspring should come to whom the promise had been made; and it was ordained by angels through an intermediary. [20] Now an intermediary implies more than one; but God is one.

1. Language

VOCABULARY—*Transgressions:* legal offenses resulting from breaking the law.

STYLE—Paul entertains a basic objection to his argument about the relation between the promise and the law in question and answer form.

2. Historical—There is nothing further here about Paul, the Galatians, or the opponents.

3. Theological—Paul now begins to deal with the crucial issue if his case is to stand. What is the purpose of the law? The rabbis taught, "The more law, the more life." Paul teaches, "The more law, the more death." If the law cannot make alive, if the law bears a curse rather

than a blessing, and if the law does not alter God's promise to Abraham, then what is its purpose?

Paul begins his answer pragmatically. The law would contradict the promise if they both achieved the same results. Then there would be two competing systems, two ways of salvation. God would be eternally schizophrenic.

The law was added, however, not because man is good-willed and needs a guide to moral perfection, "It was added because of transgressions" (3:19). It is man's sin that has brought in the law, not his success. Paul will explain this thesis in detail in the next two paragraphs.

The law also was added for a limited time period, "till the offspring [Christ] should come." And the law was given indirectly through angels and therefore cannot be identified with God himself as some tried to do, "God is one" (3:20).

So far, then, Paul has established that the law is inferior to the promise because:

1. It is later in time (3:17).
2. It was given because of transgressions (3:19).
3. It was effective only until Christ came (3:19).
4. It is distinct from God being given through angels (3:19–20).

4. Strategic—Paul now takes on the major legalistic objection to his theology: Why then the law? If it is in opposition to God's promise, why was it given? If it is God's holy revelation why does it bring a curse? Paul's reply extends to the end of chapter 3.

5. Contemporary—In an age of so much anarchy it seems dangerous to speak of the inferiority of the law. But, as it has been revealed in the highest political levels of government, the cry for law and order does not produce law and order. If law is our only recourse, history would lead us to despair. There must be more than law to hold society together and to hold us together.

6. Personal—Paul writes that the law "was added because of transgressions" (3:19). In my experience the law did not produce transgression but revealed transgression.

When I was five I was in a store with my mother at Christmastime. I spotted a roll of festive tape and wanted to take it home. My mother told me to put it back, but I put it in my pocket instead. Did my mother produce my transgression by her law, "put it back"? This would be too superficial. My desire for the tape was already stronger than the law.

I would have it at any cost. So the prohibition only revealed my selfish intention and became the instrument of its actualization. James puts it this way, "Each person is tempted when he is lured and enticed by his own desire. Then desire when it has conceived gives birth to sin" (James 1:14–15).

Galatians
3:21–22

> 21 Is the law then against the promises of God? Certainly not; for if a law had been given which could make alive, then righteousness would indeed be by the law. ²² But the scripture consigned all things to sin, that what was promised to faith in Jesus Christ might be given to those who believe.

1. Language

STYLE—Paul continues his argument with another question building on 3:19, "Is the law then against the promises of God?" His answer leads to a further explanation.

2. Historical—Again nothing here helps us to understand Paul, the Galatians, or their opponents.

3. Theological—Paul has begun to answer the question of 3:19, "Why then the law?" by, "It was added because of transgressions." He now returns to that theme with a new question, "Is the law then against the promises of God?"

As we have seen above, the legalist would hold that the Old Testament teaches two ways of salvation—promise and law, and that the law, coming later, has superseded the promise.

In denying this, if God is not to be schizophrenic, Paul must justify the giving of the law. The law cannot be a way of salvation because it cannot "make alive" (3:21). Since its absolute demand greets us only with a curse (3:10), it has been given not to produce moral perfection, but to consign "all things to sin" (3:22). In other words, the law reveals how corrupt human nature is. Calvin said that the law is a mirror in which we see ourselves. When we hear God's demand to love him with all our heart, soul, and strength and our neighbor as ourself, we are reduced to despair. We cannot do it.

Since *all* things are consigned to sin, we have no alternative but to give up even our best deeds as tainted with selfishness, and simply throw ourselves upon Christ: "that what was promised to faith in Jesus Christ might be given to those who believe." Only the drowning man will reach for the life preserver.

4. Strategic—Paul's argument is pragmatic, the law does not work to make alive (3:21). If it does not prove out as a way of salvation, then its purpose is to prepare for salvation by revealing our need of a Savior.

The very fact that the legalist has to live in perpetual fear of failure, in constant struggle for success, shows that the law does not "make alive." Thus the legalist is trying to use the law for something other than its intended purpose.

5. Contemporary—The law reveals the sinfulness, the corruption, and the impotence of all things. "The scripture consigned all things to sin" (3:22). What a blow to the ego of 20th century man.

This was to be the "Christian century." Our age was to be the climax of the evolutionary process. Science and technology were to lift our drudgery, control nature, and secure our future.

America was to be the apex of this process. We welcomed the immigrants. Our melting pot would mold the new man. Education would strip away the ignorance of the past and prepare for democracy.

"Thine alabaster cities gleam, undimmed by human tears." How shallow the old myths sound.

After a constant series of wars, depressions, recessions, and the moral failure of our leadership, we are ready again to listen to Paul, "all things to sin." Like the boys in *Lord of the Flies* we will only be saved from ourselves by outside intervention.

6. Personal—"All things to sin." How my pride fights this.

After I had stolen the Christmas tape my mother found it and took me to the store to give it back. That was one of the longest drives I have ever taken. To remember that even now makes my hands perspire. But as a British clergyman once said, "the longer you live with sin, the less you know about it." Sin is a narcotic; it dulls the conscience. We soon become sophisticated sinners. I deal with my sin through rationalization. I am not any worse than others.

Here the light of God's word must awaken me. "The *scripture* consigned all things to sin" (3:22), neither reason, nor society—but the scripture. God shows us our true condition, so that, finally Christ will be our only alternative.

Galatians
3:23–29

> 23 Now before faith came, we were confined under the law, kept under restraint until faith should be revealed. 24 So that the law was our custodian until Christ came, that we might be justified by faith. 25 But now that faith has come, we are no longer under a custodian; 26 for in Christ Jesus you are all sons of God, through faith. 27 For as many of you as were baptized into Christ have put on Christ. 28 There is neither Jew nor Greek, there is neither slave nor free, there is neither male nor female; for you are all one in Christ Jesus. 29 And if you are Christ's, then you are Abraham's offspring, heirs according to promise.

1. Language

VOCABULARY—*Custodian:* caretaker. *Sons of God:* members of God's family. *Baptized:* immersion, pouring or sprinkling with water representing cleansing from sin. *Jew, Greek:* Jew and non-Jew, the totality of humanity. *Free:* all who are not slaves.

STYLE—Paul completes his theological discussion of the law and its place in God's purpose. The style, therefore, reflects the detail of his argument and his final conclusion. The key word again is *faith*, used five times.

2. **Historical**—There is no information here to enhance our understanding of Paul or his opponents. We may infer from 3:28 that the Galatian churches contained Jews, Greeks, slaves, freemen, men and women. But these categories may also simply be comprehensive terms with no special reference to Galatia.

3. **Theological**—We have seen above that one purpose of the law

was to reveal sin (3:22). Now Paul adds a second: the law restrains sin. It confines us (3:23), being our custodian or caretaker until Christ comes (3:24). The presence of the highway patrol both reveals the speed limit and encourages us to abide by it. Such is the law.

Confinement, however, is not life. Now that Christ has come, now that faith is here, we no longer need the restraint. Christ has fulfilled the demand and judgment of the law so that we can be justified, pronounced "not guilty," before God by faith. Paul concludes, "for in Christ Jesus you are all (Jew and Gentile) sons of God through faith" (3:26).

The result of faith, then, is a new family identity, the assurance of belonging in the universe, as "sons of God." This is symbolized by baptism into Christ, a break with the old life and entrance into a new environment. It also means putting on Christ, as putting on new clothes reflects a new sense of self-worth (3:27). These pictures: baptism and new attire, are different ways in which Paul expresses the end of the old life and the beginning of the new life in Christ.

Since we are accepted before God we now find a new equality and unity with each other. The old racial barriers are broken down, "There is neither Jew nor Greek." The old social and economic barriers are broken down, "there is neither slave nor free," and the old sexual barriers are broken down, "there is neither male nor female," for "you are all one in Christ Jesus" (3:28). This oneness is equality in need, we are all sinners; equality in forgiveness, we all meet at the cross; and equality in fellowship, we all love each other and demonstrate our unity to the world.

Since we belong to Christ, we belong to the one who fulfilled the promise to Abraham, and this makes us heirs of that promised blessing. So Paul closes chapter 3.

In summary, then, the law supports the promise because it deals with sin until Christ comes to remove both sin and the restraint of the law, making the promise to Abraham available to all.

4. Strategic—Paul has contested the legalists' view of the law. The law has been given not to enhance moral life, but to reveal moral weakness. It has been given not to perfect society but by restraining sin to make society possible. Its value has now been fulfilled in Christ who forgives sin and empowers us to live a new life in community.

Returning to the law after Christ's coming, as the legalists propose, would be absurd. We would exchange the fulfillment for the preparation, the eternal for the temporary, and, in effect, deny the finality and completeness of what Christ has done. Christ plus anything is heresy.

Rather than celebrating our new identity as sons and our new unity, "all one in Christ Jesus," we would be erecting again that barrier which divides us from each other, only restraining, not canceling sin.

If we demand to work our own way to God, then we reject his free promise of blessing. We are no longer Abraham's sons, even though we are marked with Abraham's covenant. Our future is that of our own making, not the gracious inheritance promised to all "by faith."

5. **Contemporary**—We live in a miserably divided world: east against west, communists against capitalists, Jews against Arabs, whites against blacks, conservatives against liberals, adults against youth, women against men. This division is not only external, it is internal, we are divided selves.

The sign that this is not the way things were intended to be is our longing and quest for unity. We have tried political solutions: the United Nations. We have tried economic solutions: the Common Market. We have tried ideological solutions: the Marxist classless society. All to no avail.

Paul sees the only lasting unity in Christ because only in him is the moral dilemma of our alienation resolved. With guilt atoned for and sins forgiven, we are free at last not only to accept ourselves as we really are, but also to accept each other.

The Christian community is a *real* community. It is not dressed up in its "Sunday best," running through the ritual, playing church. It is a body of people who have been leveled at the cross. As Earl Palmer says, "The doctrine of the total depravity of man is a democratic doctrine—all are sinners." In this leveling, we abandon the pretense of self-righteousness for Christ's righteousness which is ours simply "by faith."

We now share a common baptism—into Christ and a common identity, we have "put on Christ." At last the barriers of race, class, and even sex are broken down. This new unity is to be embodied in the Christian community. We are to be the visible sign in this world of the reality of redemption.

Tragically enough this is too often not the case. It has been said that the most segregated hour in America is 11:00 o'clock on Sunday morning. We can easily identify the Protestant denomination by the class it ministers to. This is more a result of historical roots in immigration and cultural taste than it is a result of theological differences.

The situation of women in the church is a classic example of the violation of Galatians 3:28. Women have been relegated to serving food, caring for children, and sewing for missionaries in most congregations. In other words, they simply project their domestic duties into the local church. While the New Testament does see role differences for the sexes, this functional separation never was meant to eliminate women from spiritual and ecclesiastical responsibility. Since we are saved by faith and since there is "neither male nor female" this must be demonstrated in the local congregation.

The divisions of our world, and the longing for unity, all present an unmatched opportunity for the Christian. Now we can display in fact that Christ makes us one and that redemption has happened. If it is cold outside and warm inside, we will want to come into the warmth. Here is evangelism by being, not merely by doing.

6. **Personal**—A few years ago I became involved with Young Life, an evangelical organization in youth ministry. We worked to bring black students to California to attend college. Over three years we cared for about twenty students. In the first year two of them lived in a little house behind my office at the church. Suddenly I was confronted with a whole new culture from the streets of Harlem. I had to learn a new vocabulary, find new stations on my car radio, and run on a new time schedule. We had our tears and our laughs. We had deep moments too and began to share in a ministry of outreach to the black community. By the spring of that year we had Tuesday night basketball in our gym with the top high school and collegiate players from Southern California, including John Block, Lucius Allen, Lew Alcindor, Curtis Rowe, and Sidney Wicks who are now all professionals with the National Basketball Association. After a lot of ball we would all sit on the gym floor and I would share something of Christ.

For me the greatest results of this experiment in faith were the changes I experienced. I became more flexible, open and confident surrounded by these young men. I became more sensitive to their past and the black struggle became personal to me as they pulled on my heart.

What I discovered through all the hassles was that *in fact* not just in good theology, through Christ, "there is neither Jew nor Greek." We began to share a mission together. We prayed together. We touched each other and I could witness that Christ makes us one. The horizons of my conservative, white, middle-class upbringing were pushed back by the grace of God, and I could never pull them in completely again.

Questions for Discussion and Reflection: Chapter 3

3:1–5

1. How do I know whether or not I have the Holy Spirit?
2. What experiences of the Spirit do I have to share?
3. When was the last time I communicated "Christ crucified" to someone? What happened?
4. Why is it easy to turn back to "the flesh" in living the Christian life?

3:6–9

5. How has the character of my earthly father been reflected in me?
6. Illustrate one way that faith has been demonstrated in my Christian experience. How does this help me identify with Abraham, my "spiritual father"?
7. If I substitute *vision* for *faith* how can this help me see how God blesses me? Yeats said, "With dreams begins responsibility." How can this keep my faith from being vague and irrelevant?

3:10–14

8. How do I feel when someone "lays down the law"?
9. What evidence do I have for the existence of my conscience? How do I deal with it?
10. When I think of God as "holy" what picture comes into my mind?
11. "Some people expect more justice from the sheriff than from God." How do I react to that statement?
12. When I read that Christ became a curse for us how do I feel about this?
13. "I must either accept the atonement or repeat it." What is the truth of that statement?
14. What assurance do I have today that God's blessing is upon me?

3:15–18

15. What evidence do I have for the faithfulness of God?
16. How do I deal with apparent contradictions in my faith?
17. When circumstances deny God's promises what are my alternative reactions?

3:19–20

18. What function does the law have in my life?

19. Why is the call for "law and order" inadequate?
20. When I see a policeman following me in traffic, how do I feel?

3:21–22

21. In what way is the law a mirror within which I see myself?
22. How do I feel about the statement: "all things are tainted with selfishness"?

3:23–29

23. How do I feel about God saying "Not guilty" over my life?
24. How has my faith been demonstrated? What new clothes have I put on as a Christian?
25. How does my fellowship reflect the end of personal barriers between race, sex, and social group?
26. What new friendships do I have as a result of becoming a Christian?

4
Galatians
4:1-7

4 I mean that the heir, as long as he is a child, is no better than a slave, though he is the owner of all the estate; ² but he is under guardians and trustees until the date set by the father. ³ So with us; when we were children, we were slaves to the elemental spirits of the universe. ⁴ But when the time had fully come, God sent forth his Son, born of woman, born under the law, ⁵ to redeem those who were under the law, so that we might receive adoption as sons. ⁶ And because you are sons, God has sent the Spirit of his Son into our hearts, crying, "Abba! Father!" ⁷ So through God you are no longer a slave but a son, and if a son then an heir.

1. Language

VOCABULARY—*The elemental spirits of the universe:* the planets and astrological signs which held the fate of the nations and individuals ruled by them. They now are controlled by Satan and his fallen angels. *Adoption:* a legal change of status providing family membership not naturally deserved. *Abba:* the Aramaic family word for "Father," denoting a deeply personal relationship.

STYLE—Paul pauses to illustrate and elaborate on the theme of sonship as he concludes his theological section. The word *son* appears four times.

2. Historical—Nothing here particularly adds to our knowledge of Paul, the Galatians, or their opponents. Paul's use of the Aramaic

Abba (4:6) reveals his Jewish background, Aramaic being the spoken language of Palestine in the first century.

3. **Theological**—In 3:29 Paul has introduced a new idea: to belong to Christ and through him to Abraham means that we are now heirs. In 4:1–7, therefore, the Apostle explains what he means by this. He begins with an illustration.

Paul says that even an heir, a son, when he is a child is like a slave until he reaches adulthood. Thus he is cared for and guarded and while his future is assumed, his present is grim (4:1–2).

Likewise, during the period of law, *we,* Jews and Gentiles, were like slaves, either under the law as our custodian (3:24) or controlled by the stars, under the bondage of fate, "the elemental spirits of the universe" (4:3).

Now God has intervened. In the fullness of times he sent his Son. Here Paul implies that Christ is divine, coming from God, and unique, "his Son." The Son came not as an angelic being from heaven or as a mythological figure, he came as a man, "born of woman," and a Jew, "born under the law" (4:4). His purpose? Redemption. To break us out of the spiritual and moral bondage within which we were encased, "to redeem those who were under the law" (4:5). The result is that we have been adopted into God's new family as sons (4:5). We belong, not by our own right or accomplishment, but by God's grace.

The sign of our sonship is the entrance of God's Spirit into our lives. The Spirit allows us to call the holy God by an intimate family name, "Abba! Father!" (4:6). This is the proof positive that we belong, and that we are heirs.

For Paul the universe is fallen. Thus this evil world is dominated by guilt, despair, and death. Even God's law, which is good, now produces death because of sin. While the Jews are in bondage to its moral demand, the Gentiles are in bondage to the spiritual corruption of the universe. Both the law and the "elemental spirits" conspire against man, holding him in slavery. The bondage of the *law* is perhaps more subtle, holding out the false hope of performance—righteousness, or for the morally sensitive, simply bringing a sense of helplessness. This is one kind of bondage. The Gentile bondage to the stars, to fate brings the bondage of despair. "Why try, all is impersonally controlled and predetermined?" This bleak universe is merely the mindless rolling of the wheel of fate, and all are ultimately crushed by it.

Into this bondage, then, Christ has come, to break its grip upon us morally and spiritually. When we become Christians we receive:

1. A new position, sons (4:5).
2. A new power, the Spirit of his Son (4:6).
3. A new proof, "Abba! Father!" (4:6).
4. A new promise, heirs (4:7).

The proof of the Spirit's presence is assured to us not by the feelings we had in our conversion, not by our subsequent experiences of the Spirit, not by the gift of tongues, but by being able to call upon the Holy God as *Father*. To stand before the creator of the cosmos who holds time and eternity in his hand and say, "Daddy," can only be a result of the Spirit's work in us.

4. Strategic—Paul draws the threads of chapter 3 together here. We were in bondage. Christ has come. We are redeemed. Because of this we have a whole new quality of life and assurance.

To the legalists Paul says—you offer us slavery again. You would take us back to our childhood. But God has given us sonship, inheritance, and we will not go back. To the Galatians Paul says, you have the Spirit in you. You have experienced what I am talking about. Remember where it came from and do not go back to the old life again. Thus Paul ends as he began in 3:1–5, with the Spirit as the sign and guarantee of that which he speaks.

5. Contemporary—I was flying East recently on United Airlines and found in their magazine astrological forecasts for businessmen. I imagined that decisions would be made on Wall Street because of the position of the stars! How ironic that in our so-called "scientific age" astrology is a booming business holding the minds and hearts of millions of people. Why is this?

First, it appeals to our need to know the future. We are afraid. We are insecure. Here is secret knowledge of what is coming offered to us and we grasp it eagerly. Secondly, it appeals to our need for stability. It comes garbed in the wisdom of the ages. It presents itself as "scientific." It claims mathematical exactness. Thirdly, and most important, it works. I have no doubt that there is reality behind astrology and the occult.

In Hawaii at dinner on impulse I had my palm read by a lovely oriental woman. She had never seen me before and as she read my hand she began to relate things about me which were uncanny. When she left I was shaken, and thanked God that I was a Christian because if not, I knew I would go after her secret knowledge. The descriptions of my personality given under my astrological sign clearly describe my fundamental character. Here is a "wisdom" which turns out to be a bondage because it lures us from the living God to other Satanic powers which, at the price of our soul, will give us enough of the future to hold us, but never enough to save us. I take astrology seriously and stay away from it, but I take Christ more seriously and seek to stay close to him.

6. **Personal**—How can I know that I am a Christian? How can I have the assurance that the Holy Spirit lives in me and unites me to Christ?

I can look back on a real and dramatic conversion at the age of fifteen when I felt an overwhelming sense of release, fullness, and acceptance. The experience lasted for two weeks. I can remember conversations when God took over, providing words and thoughts I knew I did not have. I recall prayers when time and space seemed to vanish and God was almost tactility real. Do these experiences guarantee the presence of the Holy Spirit? Not for Paul. The guarantee lies in "Abba! Father!"

To know that the Father holds me; to know God is at home in his universe; to know, in the words of Malcolm Muggeridge that I am no longer a D.P., a displaced person; and to be able to say to God, *Father*, this is the guarantee. This is the sign. This is the result of Jesus' work. When you pray, pray like this, "Our Father."

Galatians
4 8–11

> 8 Formerly, when you did not know God, you were in bondage to beings that by nature are no gods; 9 but now that you have come to know God, or rather to be known by God, how can you turn back again to the weak and beggarly elemental spirits, whose slaves you want to be once more? 10 You observe days, and months, and seasons, and years! 11 I am afraid I have labored over you in vain.

1. Language

VOCABULARY—*No gods:* idols. "Observe days, and months, and seasons and years": the Jewish ritual calendar.

STYLE—Paul now turns from theology to exhortation, using both question and exclamation. He concludes with his personal feeling in 4:11 transitioning to the next section.

2. Historical—Paul tells us about the Galatians past and present. In their non-Christian state they were in bondage to *no gods,* namely idols. This means that they are largely converts not from Judaism, but the pagan world.

Now they are in danger of lapsing back into their old bondage "to the weak and beggarly elemental spirits" by a new means, through the law. They want to observe the Jewish ritual calendar. This would mean, for Paul, that his work is empty (4:11).

3. Theological—God has intervened in the Galatians' lives, setting them free from the illusions of their idolatry, the evil powers of their pagan worship. Thus, they have come to know him (4:9). Paul adds a theological corrective at this point: "or rather to be known by God," because the initiative always rests in God's hands.

If the Galatians now accept the law, here represented in the ritual calendar year (4:10), they will be going back to the old bondage from which they have been rescued. In other words, for Paul, moral bondage to the law and spiritual bondage to the stars, is still bondage just the same. This "present evil age" (1:4) is ruled by Satan, and he uses anything he can to hold us in his power. Thus, religion, morality, even the law are his tools. When we have the illusion of our own righteousness as adequate through the law, we are deluded by Satan. But as Luther says, even the Devil is God's Devil. Thus, although Satan perverts God's intention in giving the law, God is greater than Satan and his true intention that the law should bring us to Christ will triumph.

4. Strategic—Paul becomes personal again. The mixture of theological argument and exhortation keeps the letter moving. The Apostle has dealt with the bondage of the law; now he turns to the bondage of the Galatians. The contrast between their new identity as sons of God and the presence of the Spirit, and their old, empty life is striking. His marveling at their willingness to return to bondage is appropriate. His lament over the possible vanity of his work with them is understandable. All of this shows that Paul expresses various moods and uses different tactics in bringing the Galatians back to the gospel.

5. Contemporary—The Bible carries on a continual polemic against idolatry. Here Paul touches it for a moment, "beings that by nature are no gods" (4:8). The emptiness of idols rests in their inability to speak or act. They are silent and immobile. While the idol represents a real power—nature, fertility, the state—it is still in the control of man. We carry our idols with us, and we limit their power.

The modern church is curiously silent about our idols. Because they are not personified we assume they do not exist.

We can test our true worship, however. Questions such as these are relevant: How do I spend my money? What do I do with my leisure time? What do I fantasize and dream about? When I am in command of the conversation what do I bring up? What magazines do I purchase? What articles do I read? What pictures do I look at? Here I begin to see my real gods.

Sex and money, pride and power; these are the gods of our age. Can we say we have never prostrated ourselves at their altars? Dare we presume to believe that they have no attraction to us? Yes, and like the idols of old we seek to control them, rather than let them control us. How well do we succeed? The answer is written in the history of our decade. Our idols mock us for they have won us and they are "by nature no gods" (4:8).

6. Personal—Paul writes, "Now that you have come to know God, or rather to be known by God, how can you turn back again...?" (4:9). This is the ambiguity of my life, after knowing God, how can I turn back? But I do. When I am lonely, when I am under pressure, when God seems silent, when circumstances "get me down," when a crisis comes, I am tempted to "turn back."

"I was deluded," I say. I have been sold a bill of goods. "It can't be real," I protest. The whole thing is a joke, a myth, an idle hope. I cry out for that which I can touch. I reverse the words of an old hymn: "More by sight, less by faith." My body demands that its needs be met, regardless of my spirit or conscience. The old life looks alluring. Think of the fun I'm missing.

Yet, in the crisis, another voice speaks. How can you turn back? Was there any meaning before Christ? Where else have you experienced such a quality of relationships? Do you really want the old, self-destructive loneliness? Can you not trust God through this pain? Has he disappointed you before? And there is but one answer. It is Christ or suicide. Or perhaps the slower death of a coward who knows that all is ultimately futile.

Galatians
4:12–20

12 Brethren, I beseech you, become as I am, for I also have become as you are. You did me no wrong; ¹³ you know it was because of a bodily ailment that I preached the gospel to you at first; ¹⁴ and though my condition was a trial to you, you did not scorn or despise me, but received me as an angel of God, as Christ Jesus. ¹⁵ What has become of the satisfaction you felt? For I bear you witness that, if possible, you would have plucked out your eyes and given them to me. ¹⁶ Have I then become your enemy by telling you the truth? ¹⁷ They make much of you, but for no good purpose; they want to shut you out, that you may make much of them. ¹⁸ For a good purpose it is always good to be made much of, and not only when I am present with you. ¹⁹ My little children, with whom I am again in travail until Christ be formed in you! ²⁰ I could wish to be present with you now and to change my tone, for I am perplexed about you.

1. Language

STYLE—The confrontation of 4:8–11 turns to pleading in 4:12–20. Paul not only calls the Galatians *brethren* in 4:12, but *my little children* in 4:19. Once again, there is a recital of the past which now centers in the warm relationship which Paul first enjoyed with the Galatians. He is free to express his feelings, "I am again in travail" (4:19), "I am perplexed" (4:20). The style throughout is autobiographical.

2. Historical—Paul narrates his evangelistic visit. Because of a disease, perhaps malaria, the Apostle was driven into higher country and preached to the Galatians (4:13). Although his sickness was a trial, he was received as Christ himself because of the good news which he bore and the way in which he bore it (4:14).

As Paul identified with his converts (4:12), so they were profoundly moved and were ready even to pluck out their eyes for him (4:15). Does this mean that he had bad eyesight?

Now, however, things have changed. Paul's enemies have come, flattering the Galatians in order to satisfy their own ego (4:17). This has produced perplexity and travail for the Apostle. He desires to be with the Galatians, but because he cannot, he writes this letter (4:20).

3. **Theological**—Paul mentions, in passing, the secret of his evangelistic success: identification, "Brethren, I beseech you, become as I am, for I also have become as you are" (4:12).

As Paul identified with the Galatians, moving to them, caring for them, laying his life out before them, so they responded with extreme gratitude. They received him as an angel of God, even as Christ himself. They would have given their eyes to him (4:15).

On the basis of that relationship, Paul, in a mixed metaphor, experiences birth pangs until they become pregnant with Christ (4:19).

Here we see the deep emotional ties between the Apostle and his converts.

Behind Paul stands Christ himself who came and in the incarnation identified with us. Thus the word must become flesh in every generation as Christ lives his life in us.

Too often the gospel is thrown like a stone at people. It is easy to give a message, but harder to give a life. Paul gave both. It was out of the caring and sharing of himself that his message became believable. We cannot tell people that God loves them in an unloving way. As Marshall McLuhan says, "The medium is the message."

4. **Strategic**—After detailed history, closely reasoned theology, and exhortation, the time has come for appeal. Paul changes his tactics again, "Brethren, I beseech you . . ." (4:12). Rather than merely answering his opponents' arguments, or instructing in good theology, Paul must touch the heart. After blasting through the Galatians' defenses and overwhelming them with the brilliance of his mind, the Apostle falls to his knees. Pascal writes, "The heart has reasons that reason cannot know." Paul goes beyond reason to the heart.

He reminds the Galatians of his sacrifice in coming to them. He recalls their response to him in love and affection. He demonstrates that his motive for confronting them with the truth is his continuing care and concern for them. Now he feels pain and perplexity toward them (4:19–20). Such a rush of fond memory and warmth may do what good theology alone will never do. Paul uses the full range of his feelings and abilities to bring the Galatians back.

5. **Contemporary**—The simple question for evangelism today is: is it evangelism of the heart? Yes, truth must be spoken. Yes, reasons must be offered. But beyond that is our common humanity, and through this we can identify with the people to whom we go regardless of how lost or different from us they may be.

The reason this kind of evangelism is avoided is because of its cost-liness. It is much safer to bomb people with the gospel. It is much easier to limit our involvement with them to a handshake after church or a prayer letter.

When I was in high school I had a summer job in a bottled water company. As a young Christian I became concerned for the foul mouth and unhappy life of one of the woman employees, so I left an anony-mous tract in her box. To this day I do not know whether she received it or read it. But my guilt was assuaged. What I could not do because of my insecurity and fear was become involved in her life personally.

Paul, however, shows us the only real way, "I also have become as you are" (4:12). It is after the model of the incarnation that real evangelism will prosper.

6. Personal—My conversion came about through a high school evangelical organization which had mastered the principle of identifica-tion.

Rather than the Young Life leader sitting around a church waiting for us to come to him, from the model of the incarnation, he came to us. After school he watched football practice, getting to know the players. He was often seen on the campus talking with students. As a good missionary, he learned our language and came to where we were. On the basis of those friendships, those growing emotional ties, he invited us to attend an informal meeting in a home on Tuesday nights. It was not scary to go to a home. This non-institutional setting helped us to relax. The fact that we were invited to a "Young Life Club" sounded good, every high school kid wants to belong to some club.

As an insecure sophomore I was desperate to belong. My problems were social, and in the context of Young Life I discovered people who genuinely cared for me. They learned my name. They offered me a ride on Tuesday nights. They wanted me to meet Christ.

When I was told that God loved me just as I was, I could believe it because I had already seen it in the lives of those about me. It was only a short time before I gave my heart to Christ. Paul writes, "I . . . have become as you are" (4:12), and this is the evangelistic secret to which my own life bears witness.

Galatians
4:21–31

21 Tell me, you who desire to be under law, do you not hear the law? ²² For it is written that Abraham had two sons, one by a slave and one by a free woman. ²³ But the son of the slave was born according to the flesh, the son of the free woman through promise. ²⁴ Now this is an allegory: these women are two covenants. One is from Mount Sinai, bearing children for slavery; she is Hagar. ²⁵ Now Hagar is Mount Sinai in Arabia; she corresponds to the present Jerusalem, for she is in slavery with her children. ²⁶ But the Jerusalem above is free, and she is our mother. ²⁷ For it is written,

"Rejoice, O barren one that does not bear;
  break forth and shout, thou who art not in travail;
  for the desolate hath more children than she who hath a husband."

²⁸ Now we, brethren, like Isaac, are children of promise. ²⁹ But as at that time he who was born according to the flesh persecuted him who was born according to the Spirit, so it is now. ³⁰ But what does the scripture say? "Cast out the slave and her son; for the son of the slave shall not inherit with the son of the free woman." ³¹ So, brethren, we are not children of the slave but of the free woman.

1. Language

VOCABULARY—*Abraham:* the Father of the Jewish race, see Galatians 3:6 ff, and Genesis 12:1 ff. *Allegory:* an account where the people and places have another meaning beyond the historical, where they represent another, higher truth. *Mount Sinai:* The mountain from which God gave the law through Moses, see Exodus 19:1–20:20. *Hagar:* the Egyptian maid of Abraham's wife Sarah, see Genesis 16:1. *Jerusalem:* The holy city, David's city, the capital of Israel. *Isaac:* Abraham's own legitimate son born in his old age, see Genesis 21:1–3.

STYLE—Paul presents an allegorical interpretation of the story of Abraham and his two sons. This approach to the Old Testament is typical of the Jewish Rabbis and contrasts with Paul's regular historical approach, see Galatians 3:6 ff.

2. Historical—Paul tells us that he is addressing those in Galatia

who desire to be under the law (4:21). He also alludes to persecution by the legalists (4:29). Otherwise, this passage tells us nothing of him or his opponents.

3. Theological—Although Paul usually views the Old Testament historically, he offers here one of his rare examples of allegory, changing his tactics. He builds on the two sons Abraham fathered. This is apt, as we have seen, because Abraham is the founder of the Jewish race (3:6 ff).

The Apostle begins by briefly reconstructing the story (4:22–23). Abraham had two sons, Ishmael and Isaac. Ishmael was born through Abraham's slave Hagar in the attempt to provide an heir in his old age while his wife was barren. This act was "according to the flesh" (4:23) because God had promised Abraham a son (Genesis 15:4), but now he tried to take things into his own hands. God's promise held true, despite Ishmael, and Isaac was eventually born from Sarah in her old age as the son of God's promise (4:23). In this Paul sees a deeper allegorical truth relating to the whole discussion of law and grace.

The maid, Hagar, Abraham's slave, represents the covenant of law, Mount Sinai where Moses received the law. This Paul connects to the earthly Jerusalem which is still in bondage to the Jewish law. As Ishmael, Hagar's son, persecuted Isaac, so those who share in God's promise to Abraham are persecuted by the legalists today (4:28–29).

Isaac, however, was born according to God's promise to give Abraham his own heir. Thus he identified, not with the earthly Jerusalem, in bondage to the law, but with the heavenly Jerusalem which is free in the grace of God.

God's judgment is sure; the slave son, Ishmael, the son of the flesh and the law, will be cast out (4:30). Only the free son, Isaac and his descendants, will inherit the promise and be welcomed into the heavenly Jerusalem.

What are we to make of this? In the first place, the allegory is built upon Paul's historical–theological exposition of Abraham in 3:6–9. Second, Paul holds to the historical core because, in fact, Abraham did receive the promise of God's blessing to the nations in which we all share by faith. In the third place, Abraham's attempt to secure an heir through Hagar is an excellent example of not trusting God and acting in the flesh as the legalists do. Fourth, Isaac stands as a witness to God's grace giving Abraham a son when his resources were exhausted (compare Romans 4:13–25). Thus, this is not "wild allegory," but an interpretation of the Old Testament under historical control.

Paul can jump from Ishmael to Sinai to Jerusalem to the legalists because he sees two kinds of history running throughout time—the flesh and the Spirit, works and faith, law and grace. In principle they provide the continuity between each generation. Either we trust God or we do not, and in that decision we belong to Isaac or Ishmael. Thus, while allegory seems farfetched at times, the principles behind it in Paul's usage stand.

4. Strategic—The Apostle's transition is abrupt. After entreaty he suddenly launches into a detailed allegory. Why this change?

In effect Paul is saying to the legalists, "All right, you who want to follow the law, if you try to argue your case from the Old Testament, well, so will I. If you bring in allegory to aid in your case, then so can I. If you are Jewish in your approach to the Galatians, I can out-Jewish you any day and I will prove it now from Abraham and his sons."

What we see here, again, is more of the full range of Paul's argument. To his confrontation, his historical defense, his appeal to experience, his theological exposition, his rebuke, his pleading, he now adds allegory. The Apostle is firing all his ammunition. No possibility will be overlooked. If he cannot win them with one argument, he will win them with another.

To legalistic opponents using the Old Testament, this allegory becomes a telling refutation, and thus it stands in an important place in Paul's argument.

5. Contemporary—Paul sees, as we have shown, history running on two conflicting levels—the flesh and the Spirit. Here is an inner continuity available only to the man with spiritual perception. Secular historians see only fleshly history and are impressed. Christians must see the spiritual aspect which makes true, lasting history.

Toynbee, I believe, chronicled twenty-six civilizations. Is there no continuity beyond the ebb and flow of mortal accomplishment? How can we connect Israel, the Roman Empire, the Dark and Middle Ages, the Renaissance and Reformation, the Enlightenment, the rise of the modern states, the Industrial Revolution, the era of colonization, and the decline of the West? Is there not a spiritual continuity throughout evidencing the judgment and redemption of the living God?

Let me give a contemporary example. In the fall of 1973, the Davis Cup tennis finals were played in Bucharest between the United States and Rumania. It was a classic athletic confrontation between East and West. With drama and perseverance the United States won. The victory was hailed and reported extensively in the press. But unknown and unreported was the drama of the spiritual struggle going on in the life of Dennis Ralston, the captain of the U.S. Davis Cup team. Dennis' wife had recently become a Christian. Now he was engaged himself in a spiritual search. The pressure of Bucharest brought him to the point of praying seriously for the first time in his life. At the same time, the number one player for the U.S., Stan Smith, was a Christian, and he and Dennis found a fellowship under the pressure of that match which they had never had before.

The athletic world knew only of the drama of the U.S. victory. That is history after the flesh, only a memory and soon to be forgotten. But the spiritual drama in Dennis Ralston's confrontation with Jesus Christ endured. That is history after the Spirit which extends into eternity.

6. Personal—In my life there is history after the flesh and history after the Spirit. The flesh is easy and obvious: my birth, education, employment, honors, books, and articles. But the true history, the history after the Spirit is much more complex. It is a history of inner conflicts and God's intervention, of the oscillation between doubt and trust, of retreat and advance. It is a history of relationships, some chosen, most by surprise. It is a history of temptation, failure, forgiveness, struggle, and growth. It is a history of trust, often inspite of empirical evidence. It is a history of seeing the unseen, of light in the darkness, and of never-ceasing love, an open hand from heaven welcoming the pilgrim home.

History after the Spirit is real history. History after the flesh is only a sham, soon to be buried under the pyramids of our illusions, guarded by the silent Sphinx, fitting monument to its enigma.

Questions for Discussion and Reflection: Chapter 4

4:1–7

1. When I think about my future, what comes to mind?
2. What does it mean to be an *heir*?
3. When I hear the word *father* what comes to mind? How has my reaction to this word been conditioned by my earthly father?
4. Why is being able to call God *Father* the ultimate test of the Spirit's presence in me? How do I feel about this?

4:8–11

5. Why is religion *bondage*?

6. What are the idols of my life? How do I worship them? How can I reject them?
7. Why am I tempted to reenthrone my old idols?

4:12–20

8. Who am I identifying with for the sake of Christ?
9. Who is identifying with me to learn more of Christ?
10. Who has had "birth pangs" for me?
11. For whom have I had "birth pangs?"
12. Can I be a victorious Christian and be perplexed? Explain.

4:21–31

13. How do I describe my history "after the flesh"?
14. How do I describe my history "after the Spirit"?
15. Which history is most important to me? How do I demonstrate that importance?

5

Galatians

5:1

5 For freedom Christ has set us free; stand fast therefore, and do not submit again to a yoke of slavery.

1. Language

VOCABULARY—*A yoke of slavery:* Paul's word play with a favorite Jewish metaphor describing the law as a yoke.

STYLE—Strong exhortation and warning which introduces the section on the practical Christian life in chapters 5 and 6.

2. Historical—Nothing is added to our knowledge of Paul, the Galatians, or their opponents, except the word *again* which means that the Galatians were once in bondage, but now have been set free.

3. Theological—Freedom is the reality of the Christian life, "Christ has set us free," and the goal of the Christian life, "for freedom." Nothing could be more emphatic. Christian existence can be described in many ways; here Paul comprehensively uses the word *freedom.*

Christian freedom is both negative and positive. The negative, "Christ has set us free," includes liberation from bondage to the law and its curse, the stars, Satanic power, ourselves and this present evil age. The positive, "For freedom Christ has set us free," means that we are free for God, for each other, for this world, for the future. Since that which dehumanizes us has been removed, we are now at liberty to discover our true humanity which God intended in our creation.

To surrender this freedom, then, is to surrender ourselves. It is to return to our childish existence under the law. It is to give up the maturing responsibility of making our own decisions. It is to forfeit a personal life with God for an impersonal life of rules. No wonder Paul calls us to our freedom.

Because we have been set free "for freedom," we are to stand fast in it and reject any return to legal or astrological bondage. Such a return would contradict the purpose for which Christ has freed us.

The ethical results of Christ's act must be consistent with the freedom which he has given. Paul, throughout chapters 5 and 6 will define the nature of that freedom.

4. Strategic—Encompassing the Christian life as *freedom* denies any place for the law. To "submit again to a yoke of slavery" would be to nullify the meaning of Christ's work, setting us free.

With the metaphor of the *yoke,* Paul jabs at the legalists. The Jews called men to take upon themselves the "yoke of the law." Paul attacks such an act as enslavement.

5. Contemporary—For the anarchist, freedom is unbridled self-expression, self-actualization regardless of its consequences. A recent song popularized by the late Janis Joplin says, "Freedom's just another word for nothing left to lose." Carried to an extreme, such a view of freedom becomes self-destructive, and the increase of suicide in our country is grim evidence of such freedom.

For the Marxist, freedom is insight into the predetermined processes of history and the decision to participate in them. Those who refuse, the unfree, will be crushed by them. Since the classless society is where history is going, the true revolutionary, the truly free man, is the one who joins in this unalterable movement.

For the existentialist, freedom is the affirmation of one's selfhood. In a meaningless world where we are all becoming, the free man accepts responsibility for himself and carves out his own destiny by the personal decisions he makes. In effect, he creates his own nature by deciding to be what he is.

Against these distortions the Christian affirms true freedom. Each view has a truth: the anarchist realizes that there is no meaning or security in this world's order, the Marxist realizes that man must participate in a meaning greater than himself, and the existentialist realizes that we must accept responsibility for who we are. The fallacy in these distortions, however, is the failure to see man made in God's image. In creation God has given us a relationship with himself and a destiny in this world which are ingrained. Although we may deny this because of sin, we will only be truly free when we know God. As Augustine put it, "Lord, thou hast made us for thyself and our hearts are restless until they rest in thee." Thus freedom is both "freedom from" and "freedom for."

The ultimate cause of our bondage is our moral failure which results in separation from the source and meaning of life. Only in Christ is this moral failure resolved, and therefore only in Christ can true freedom be found. This freedom will be expressed in positive, creative relationships, and thus bear within itself the sign of health.

6. Personal—I can never read this verse without remembering an incident when it came alive for me. As a young, single clergyman, I had been extremely careful in my relationships with girls, avoiding any hint of scandal.

Cheryl came into my life having spent two years on the Sunset Strip. There she became pregnant and, covered with guilt, came to our church to meet Christ. She was my first "Hippie."

The Sunday following her conversion she returned to church. Spotting me across a patio where scores of adults stood talking, Cheryl let out a scream, ran to me, threw her arms around me and kissed me right on the mouth.

I remember that I felt as if my head turned 360° looking for Elders as every muscle tensed. Later I realized that while I had a gospel of freedom, Cheryl was free. True, her behavior was a bit bizarre and she soon calmed down, but she was being herself. I was the one too insecure to let her be the little girl she was. *"For freedom* Christ has set us free." The verse now came home with new punch. Through people such as Cheryl God has chipped away at my defenses and helped me to relax in his love.

Galatians
5:2–12

2 Now I, Paul, say to you that if you receive circumcision, Christ will be of no advantage to you. ³ I testify again to every man who receives circumcision that he is bound to keep the whole law. ⁴ You are severed from Christ, you who would

be justified by the law; you have fallen away from grace. ⁵ For through the Spirit, by faith, we wait for the hope of righteousness. ⁶ For in Christ Jesus neither circumcision nor uncircumcision is of any avail, but faith working through love. ⁷ You were running well; who hindered you from obeying the truth? ⁸ This persuasion is not from him who called you. ⁹ A little leaven leavens the whole lump. ¹⁰ I have confidence in the Lord that you will take no other view than mine; and he who is troubling you will bear his judgment, whoever he is. ¹¹ But if I, brethren, still preach circumcision, why am I still persecuted? In that case the stumbling block of the cross has been removed. ¹² I wish those who unsettle you would mutilate themselves!

1. Language

VOCABULARY—*Leaven:* yeast which permeates dough, making it rise.

STYLE—We could call this section "polemic exhortation." For emphasis, Paul reintroduces himself in 5:2. "Now I, Paul, say . . . ." This emphatic tone continues with the solemn, "I testify again to every man . . ." (5:3). The Apostle's warnings are blunt, "You are severed from Christ . . . you have fallen away from grace" (5:4). His direct speech appears again in 5:7, "You were running well . . ."

Paul also uses questions: "Who hindered you?" (5:7); "Why am I still persecuted?" (5:11); and exclamations, "I wish those who unsettle you would mutilate themselves!" (5:12). Thus, this section is confrontive and fast-moving. Note the use of the triad, faith, hope, and love in 5:5-6.

2. Historical—The nature of Paul's opponents now fully emerges. Since they are demanding that the Galatians be circumcised (5:2), they may be properly labeled as "Judaizers." They hinder the Galatians from obeying the truth (5:7) and are troubling them (5:10).

The Apostle's conditional sentence, "If you receive circumcision . . ." (5:2) suggests that his churches have not yet capitulated. But even if they have, it makes no difference, "For in Christ Jesus neither circumcision nor uncircumcision is of any avail . . ." (5:6). While the Apostle commends them for their past, "You were running well" (5:7), he is disappointed in their present.

Perhaps the legalists charge that Paul preaches circumcision when convenient and freedom from the law when convenient (5:11). In other words, he is a hypocrite, only desiring to make fast converts, regardless of the truth. This the Apostle emphatically denies. He expresses confidence in the Galatians (5:10) and bitter judgment on their opponents, asking them, rather than seeking to circumcise others, to mutilate themselves (5:12). At the same time, Paul is confident that the Galatians will support him (5:10).

3. **Theological**—Paul argues against circumcision as an issue of principle, not of convention or convenience. The charge that he still preaches circumcision, as in his old Jewish days, is absurd, because if he did, he would be flattering egos ("You can do this for God"), and avoiding the stumbling block of the cross ("You can do nothing for God") which places him under continual persecution (5:11).

If the Galatians accept circumcision as the sign of the Old Testament law, then they lose their advantage in Christ (5:2). This is the principle at stake, for if they accept the law, they must keep it *all* (5:3), which puts them under the curse (3:10).

Thus, as their performance comes between themselves and Christ, this cuts them off from him (5:4). Taking on the law, they have fallen from grace (5:4). Rather than waiting for the "hope of righteousness" which is not only God's acceptance of them now (justification), but the perfection of their lives before him (sanctification), they are seeking to produce their own righteousness by legal observance. Either they must work their way, or let faith work through love (5:6).

The theological difficulty of this passage lies in its apparent teaching that we can lose our salvation. "If you receive circumcision, Christ will be of no advantage to you. . . . You are severed from Christ, you who would be justified by the law; you have fallen away from grace" (5:2–4).

The question is: Should we take this ultimately, that is, that if we go under the law all is lost forever, or practically, that if we go under the law while God's attitude toward us has not changed, our attitude toward him has. In other words, is it an issue of salvation or fellowship? In favor of the first position is the direct and unmodified language Paul uses. In favor of the second is that it is the Galatians who are changing their position in receiving circumcision and accepting the law. They are erecting a barrier between themselves and Christ, and the implication is that even if they have done this it does not matter, if they come back to faith (5:6). They can fall from grace, but grace will not fall from them.

As we have said, Christ plus anything is heresy. If the law is introduced we have two opposing forces in conflict with each other. Oil and water, by their molecular structure, cannot mix. We cannot serve a system and love a person at the same time.

The problem of Paul's direct language stands, however, and if there were not an eternal danger in embracing the law, then it is hard to understand the white-heat argument of this letter.

While we must ultimately trust the grace of God and rest in that, we must also guard against anything that would compromise grace and become a barrier between ourselves and Christ. When we arrive at heaven's gates it will all be by grace, but this must not lead to presumption. If we have truly been saved we are now responsible to guard the purity and truth of that salvation, ever trusting God alone for the outcome. Such is the paradox of Christian existence: grace will triumph, but responsibility is still ours. What appears to be a conflict in our minds is resolved in the mind of God. Our finitude is no match for his infinite truth. Both grace and responsibility are truths verified in our experience.

4. **Strategic**—Paul brings the subject of himself, "Now I, Paul," and his argument down upon the Galatians. The legalists have said, "Now that you have accepted Christ, go all the way. Become a complete Christian, Old and New Testament, be circumcised and keep the law." Paul says, "No!" If you are circumcised you are cut off from Christ. The very thing claimed to complete your faith will destroy it. The continuity between Old and New Testaments lies, not in law and grace, but in faith which makes us all sons of Abraham.

At the same time, we should not only fear the lapse into legalism, but also desire benefits from Christ. Paul's attack against erecting the law is balanced by the positive teaching about faith, hope (5:5), and love (5:6).

The Apostle warns and promises. He expresses confidence (5:10) and anger (5:12). He answers the slander that he preaches circumcision when convenient by displaying his suffering for the gospel (5:11). Once again we see the many tactics of Paul for winning the battle.

5. **Contemporary**—Modern legalists lack moral seriousness as did Paul's opponents in Galatia. They use the law to promote an appearance of morality. They embrace the law to salve a guilty conscience, and file off its edges with bland moralisms. They erect a standard which justifies their own behavior, and are thereby relieved at their goodness (and not

a little impressed.) Or they pursue a private ethic which is rigorous and a business ethic which is determined by the profit motive. Paul says to us all, if we accept even one part of the code we are saddled with the whole. "I testify again to every man who receives circumcision that he is bound to keep the whole law" (5:3).

I recall Bill Antablin, who worked for years with university students, saying, "Most students have few intellectual problems. They have moral problems, and when their moral life contradicts their theology either they have to bring their life up to the level of their theology or their theology down to the level of their life." This has become, in the last generation, a national pastime.

For Paul, however, God is holy and we cannot choose which of his laws we shall keep according to our fancy. The ritual law and the moral law are one. How we are to worship and how we are to behave are both important to God (and interrelated).

When the standard is the highest, then the need is the greatest and the gospel shines all the more brightly. If we offer the world a little law and a little Christ, there will be a little salvation, and we will wonder why it did not take.

Moral relativism, designed to excuse our behavior, is a deadly illusion. It only stalls my disaster. Moral absolutism forces me to face the reality of my sin and God's character. I can no longer push things into the basement of my subconscious. At the same time, in Christ, moral absolutism draws me to the only final solution. When all of God's law is heard and the cross proclaimed, I find, in the words of Karl Barth, "Total help for total need."

6. Personal—During my college days I experienced a period of intense legalism where performance for acceptance was the standard of the group. Because of my insecurities, I easily capitulated.

What I found was a diminishing of my love for Christ. Rules and regulations, the acceptance of my fellow Christians, "goodness," narrowly defined, became my preoccupation. Subtly, Christ became the means to these other things rather than the end and goal of all. My focus was on clear morality and strict orthodoxy, rather than on the Christ of clear and healthy morality and true theology.

The absurdity of this was that my exterior life was controllable, but my interior life, my needs, desires, and passions were not only uncontrolled, but fed my pride as a good Christian. By denying my needs externally, they only reverted to my dreams and fantasies. Rather than confessing my sins, facing them and dealing with them, my rigorousness only led to their returning to haunt me sevenfold.

Paul says we are bound "to keep the whole law" (5:3). But I only kept half the law—the external image of a good Christian. In this I justified myself, and my supposed goodness and pride separated me from the real Christ who is known only in the total demand of the law where he then is welcomed as total forgiveness and grace.

Galatians
5:13–15

13 For you were called to freedom, brethren; only do not use your freedom as an opportunity for the flesh, but through love be servants of one another. ¹⁴ For the whole law is fulfilled in one word, "You shall love your neighbor as yourself." ¹⁵ But if you bite and devour one another take heed that you are not consumed by one another.

1. Language

STYLE—Paul continues his exhortation on the theme of freedom for love. He uses both negative and positive statements as well as an Old Testament quotation for clarification. The key word is *love,* appearing in 5:13 and 5:14.

2. Historical—Nothing new is offered here about Paul, the Galatians, or the opponents.

3. Theological—What is the content of the freedom to which we are called? Paul answers first with a negative: "Only do not use your freedom as an opportunity for the flesh" (5:13). Christian freedom is not libertinism. Freedom in Christ is not an excuse for our selfishness. By "the flesh" Paul means our natural life separated from God, not merely physical existence. (See the works of the flesh in 5:19 ff.) We cannot live selfishly presuming that God will forgive us. Paul then answers the question of freedom with a positive, "but through love be servants of one another."

Here is the content of our freedom. Faith expresses itself, its reality in love (5:6), and love expresses itself in service. Thus the sign of faith is loving service, and this is our freedom actualized. Paul says that God signs his name to this by quoting from the Old Testament. "For the whole law is fulfilled in one word, 'You shall love your neighbor as yourself' " (5:14; Leviticus 19:18).

Legalism, then, for Paul is transformed by love. The law operates on the outside, love on the inside. The law demands, love desires.

By summarizing the law in the command to love our neighbor, Paul supports the goal of the law. If we loved perfectly, we would not lie, covet, lust, or murder. Thus Paul's argument is not with the intention of the law, but with the way of fulfilling its intention.

Either we strive to live up to the law, or we accept Christ as the one who has perfectly done that. Then, with his Spirit within us, we discover a new desire to fulfill its demand, not to gain heaven, but to demonstrate that heaven has gained us.

The word *servants* is actually stronger translated *slaves*. Love means giving ourselves to meet the needs of those around us, our neighbors. As the Good Samaritan stopped beside the road, so we must stop and respond to the needs we find. Jesus washed his disciples' feet to model their service to each other (John 13:14–15). We are called into the foot-washing business.

The opposite of this kind of love is the biting and devouring which may well be going on in Galatia (5:15). This can only lead to the ruin of the church. When the law comes in, it brings jealousy, competition, performance, guilt, and pride.

Paul's crucial assumption is that God has made man to live a life of perfect fellowship with him and his neighbor. Because of sin man can no longer fulfill that intention. The law reveals and restrains sin. Christ changes the sinner into one who loves and serves and who finds in this new life-style the fulfillment of his destiny when God created him.

4. Strategic—The objection to Paul's theology is that freedom leads to sin; if we lift the law we will have anarchy. Thus the Apostle must define what he means by freedom and show that Christian freedom fulfills the purpose of the law as the law could never do. His quote from Leviticus 19:18, "You shall love your neighbor as yourself" is apt. Here from the law Paul confounds the legalists. Serving love means that the law is being lived naturally and spontaneously as God originally intended for man.

At the same time, if the law is reintroduced, there will only be biting and devouring, rather than completed righteousness. The legalists assert that the law matures faith. Paul warns that the law will consume faith.

5. **Contemporary**—How is the faith to be expressed? What is the sign of our discipleship? Building on John 13:35, "By this all men will know that you are my disciples, if you have love for one another," Paul establishes that our orthodoxy is manifested in loving service.

The sign of faith for the Jew is righteousness. The sign of faith for the Buddhist is compassion. The sign of faith for the Muslim is submission to the will of Allah. The sign of faith for the Christian is self-giving love to our neighbor.

How easy it is to find some substitution for this sign. We propose that Christians will be known by their negative life-style: what they do not do. We assert that Christians will be known by their creedal fidelity, or their fervent witness, or their spiritual euphoria. The Bible says we shall be known by our love.

Henrietta Mears used to say that the world is looking for a drop of love. A seminary student responded, "Miss Mears, you are wrong, the world is looking for a bucketful!"

I look for the day that the world will pass by the church and say, "We can't understand how they can believe those crazy things, and we can't believe that they could sing those songs, but we can't get over how they love each other." This is the infallible sign (1 Corinthians 13).

6. **Personal**—It is a very humbling experience to be served. Simply serving others may be an ego trip. To both serve and to be served is the sign of Christ's presence, "Through love be servants of one another."

One of my closest friends was leaving for military service and during the course of our final evening together, he did a strange thing. Getting down on his knees he began to untie my shoes. At first I did not understand, and then it hit me. He began to wash my feet. I felt like protesting like Peter (John 13:6). I was embarrassed. My feet smelled. Then a great sense of love and humility flooded over me. There was nothing which I could do but let him continue, and by that act I was undone. He was serving me, kneeling before me. His humility humbled me. It was a precious moment.

This symbolic act is the fabric of our Christian community, and it is often menial, dirty business. But Jesus has come to perform menial, dirty business for us. In his love we are liberated to love each other in the same way. Now I must ask myself, "Whose feet am I washing?" Only in this way am I not a blasphemer of Christ's good name.

Galatians
5:16–24

16 But I say, walk by the Spirit, and do not gratify the desires of the flesh. [17] For the desires of the flesh are against the Spirit, and the desires of the Spirit are against the flesh; for these are opposed to each other, to prevent you from doing what you would. [18] But if you are led by the Spirit you are not under the law. [19] Now the works of the flesh are plain: immorality, impurity, licentiousness, [20] idolatry, sorcery, enmity, strife, jealousy, anger, selfishness, dissension, party spirit, [21] envy, drunkenness, carousing, and the like. I warn you, as I warned you before, that those who do such things shall not inherit the kingdom of God. [22] But the fruit of the Spirit is love, joy, peace, patience, kindness, goodness, faithfulness, [23] gentleness, self-control; against such there is no law. [24] And those who belong to Christ Jesus have crucified the flesh with its passions and desires.

1. Language

VOCABULARY—*Immorality:* unlawful sexual intercourse. *Impurity:* any sexual vice. *Licentiousness:* indecent conduct, whether or not a person is violated. *Idolatry:* any substitution for worshiping the one God. *Sorcery:* witchcraft which employs the use of drugs, casting spells on people. *Enmity:* hostility regardless of how it is manifested. *Strife:* rivalry between two people. *Jealousy:* the eager desire to possess what another has. *Anger:* an outburst of hostile feeling. *Selfishness:* self-seeking, selfish devotion to one's own interests. *Dissension:* disagreement. *Party spirit:* division of sentiment which forms a sect. *Envy:* similar to jealousy, denoting specific forms of envious desire. *Drunkenness:* overindulgence in alcohol. *Carousing:* the reveling which results from drunkenness. *The Kingdom of God:* here, God's ultimate, perfect rule and sovereignty over all things.

Love: self-giving *(agape)* care for others. *Joy:* gladness of spirit. *Peace:* spiritual well-being, wholeness. *Patience:* persistence, steadfastness. *Kindness:* generosity. *Goodness:* moral character. *Faithfulness:* fidelity to one's fellow man, consistency. *Gentleness:* sensitivity in dealing with others, warmth. *Self-control:* the mastery of one's desires and impulses.

STYLE—Paul continues with explanatory exhortation. "But I say"

(5:16), stresses his authority to offer his imperatives. In the context of the warfare of flesh and Spirit, the Apostle gives a shotgun blast of vices and virtues meant to be both comprehensive and specific. The exhortative style continues in 5:21, "I warn you, as I warned you before . . ."

2. Historical—The only concrete historical note here is in 5:21, "as I warned you before." This assures us that Paul not only evangelized the Galatians, but also instructed them in their new life.

3. Theological—Paul offers a third alternative to legalism and license, namely, "walking by the Spirit." To become a Christian means to identify with the death of Christ, to surrender the old selfish life, to accept as "dead" our this-worldly existence, life merely lived on the human level. "And those who belong to Christ Jesus have crucified the flesh with its passions and desires" (5:24). At the same time, however, we are not sinless or perfect; only Christ is. The warfare begins when we accept Christ, because now the Spirit of God gives us a spiritual nature and dwells within our old fleshly life. We are set free from the bondage of sin and now can make an authentic choice whether or not to continue in sin and gratify the flesh or to yield to the Spirit and allow him to work in us.

Before we accepted Christ we were only free to sin (however sophisticated we were at it). After we accept Christ we are free not to sin.

Thus, as far as we identify with the crucified Christ we are dead to sin (5:24), but as far as we identify with our old life sin still lives in us.

In the context of this battle, then, we work out our new life.

The flesh still makes its demands for gratification (5:16). We are tempted to egotism, sexual lust and materialism. But a new desire is at work in us, that of the Spirit, against the old desire of the flesh. The two desires fight within, demanding our allegiance. They stand in absolute opposition to each other (5:17).

What is the resolution? To say to sin, "You are crucified with Christ" (2:20, 5:24). To say to the Spirit, "Be the sovereign teacher and control of my life." "But if you are led by the Spirit you are not under the law" (5:18).

Paul now shows us exactly what he means by the warfare of the flesh and Spirit by two lists.

Appropriately he calls the first "the works of the flesh" (5:19). This is what we do by our own selfish will. The second is called "the fruit of the Spirit" (5:22). This is what the Spirit does in us when we are surrendered to him.

Both lists are similar in this sense: They exhibit the reality of flesh or Spirit in human relationships. Our nature is revealed in what it produces, and life in the flesh is a life of bitter conflict stemming from our selfishness. The works of the flesh are exhibited in *sexual sins:* immorality, impurity and licentiousness; in *false spiritualism:* idolatry, sorcery; in the *breakdown of community:* enmity, strife, jealousy, selfishness, dissension, party spirit, envy; and in *social sins:* drunkenness, carousing and the like. What Paul describes here is a life-style in the flesh. There is no grading. A jealous woman is as bad as an adulterer. A man who creates a faction is as bad as a drunk. At the same time, the list must be viewed comprehensively; this is a total lifestyle of separation from God: "Those who do such things shall not inherit the kingdom of God" (5:21). Thus, if a Christian is tempted by one of these sins or falls, this does not mean that he has lost his salvation. If the list, however, describes his life-style, he could never inherit God's kingdom because he is not exhibiting God's rule now in his behavior.

When, however, we identify with Christ in his death and open ourselves to his Spirit, fruit appears in our life which is nothing less than Christ's character being formed in us (5:22–23). Again, this new life is exhibited in relationships where out of the self-giving, gladness and wholeness of our lives (love, joy, and peace), we are now able to care for others as Christ cares. This is the loving service of the law's fulfillment in action through us (5:13). Our new character, along with the Spirit's assurance that God is our father (4:6), is the sign of truly being a Christian.

Our life is one constant decision:

1. Do I know identify with Christ's death and give up my 'natural' life at the cross?
2. Do I now yield myself to the control of the Spirit?
3. Do I now resist the demands of the flesh for selfish gratification?
4. Do I now actualize the Spirit's presence in the way in which I relate to those about me in self-giving love?

4. Strategic—Paul again demonstrates the futility of the law to produce its intended results. The law can neither engender life in the Spirit (5:18) nor oppose the results of the Spirit's work (5:23).

To go under the law, however, is at best to bridle the works of the flesh. Only the Spirit can deal with the flesh from which these evil deeds come.

Thus, the legalists are shown as unable to produce the righteous life they claim. Even if their intentions are good, they cannot reach them.

5. **Contemporary**—How easy it is in the church to pick our sins. We identify the obvious: sexual immorality and drunkenness, and avoid these easily. Those who do not are drummed out.

At the same time, we overlook the sins of character: "enmity, strife, jealousy, anger, selfishness, dissension, party spirit, envy" (5:20), or worse, we glorify them. Our strife and party spirit are spiritualized as being stalwart for the truth of the gospel. Our possessive jealousy is defended as guarding our converts from perversion. We use prayer requests as the vehicle for gossip and strife. Churches compete with each other for converts and programs, all in the name of Christ.

Paul puts the sins of the body, mind and heart together. They are all "of the flesh" when they separate us from each other, turning people into objects to be manipulated or abused. Again, the truth of the gospel will be manifested in the quality of our relationships.

One timely word invites a special comment: "sorcery" (5:20). The Greek original is the same word from which we get "pharmacy." It means "drugs," and is related to witchcraft because witches used drugs in casting spells on people. By the inclusion of this word here, Paul prohibits the use of drugs for "tripping out," for "mind expansion." To surrender myself to the control of drugs is to live in the flesh, seeking even a spiritual experience in an inauthentic way. Rather, the Spirit will expand my mind and give me a real spiritual experience with which no drug can compete.

6. **Personal**—The promise of this passage to me is that as I yield to the Spirit, Christ's character is being formed in me (5:22–23). I must affirm that character.

How easily I am hung up on my problems. How often I see my failure in relationships. How tempted I am to withdraw in discouragement, or to force myself on people all the more because of my insecurities.

God says, "By faith believe that my character is in you and being expressed through you." One source of discouragement for me is spiritual introspection. When I survey myself I find so much lust and greed, so many mixed motives. But this is exactly the problem. I cannot really survey myself. As long as I look for the fruit of the Spirit I will not find it; my eyes are in the wrong place. When I turn again to Christ, I forget myself. As I see him and become preoccupied with him, his promise is that the fruit will appear. In fellowship with Christ the "love, joy and peace" comes.

Often I have had people thank me for helping them or speak of my Christian life with praise. I think to myself, "What a hypocrite, I have fooled them." But then, another possibility is there. As I forget myself and focus on Christ, they see him in me. I am not conscious of this, but they see the other, spiritual reality in my life. Over the years I have come to accept that this is actually the case. What a relief. I do not have to perform, but yield. The promise holds, Christ will live *his* life through me and it is *his* life.

Galatians
5:25–26

25 If we live by the Spirit, let us walk by the Spirit. ²⁶ Let us have no self-conceit, no provoking of one another, no envy of one another.

1. Language

STYLE—*Let us . . . let us,* Paul continues his exhortation. This appears first as a positive in 5:25 and then three negatives in 5:26.

2. History—Nothing more is given here about Paul, the Galatians, or their opponents.

3. Theological—"If we live by the Spirit" concludes this section denoting a real condition. We could paraphrase it, "since we live by the Spirit." This, Paul has proven as early as 3:1–5. If, then, the Spirit is the author of life, the Spirit must be the means of sustaining that life: "Let us also walk by the Spirit." The Apostle has defined that walk as the Spirit's leadership (5:18) producing Christ's character (5:22–23). The metaphor of a walk is a common Biblical way of expressing the Christian life. It is placing one foot before the other to reach our destination.

This "walk by the Spirit" stands in opposition to self-conceit, provoking one another (see 5:19–21). In other words, walking by the Spirit means dependence upon Christ, not self-conceit through our own accomplishment. Walking by the Spirit means loving service, not provoking each other through competitive pride. Walking by the Spirit means accepting each other, not rejecting each other because of jealousy.

Since the Christian life is begun in the Spirit (3:3), it must be sustained by the Spirit (5:25), trusting the Spirit to bring us to our final goal.

4. Strategic—The polemic implications of these verses lie in the law's producing self-conceit, provoking and envy. Once the legal standard is reintroduced, our relationships collapse. We become busy comparing our lives and their moral and spiritual accomplishment with each other, rather than with Christ. Only by living and walking by the Spirit is authentic community possible.

5. Contemporary—The world views the Christian life as one of rigorous morality and religious ritual under the sanction of institutional authority. In this there is no difference between the church and first-century Judaism.

Paul views the Christian life as a surrender to the Spirit, and a dependence upon the Spirit, making a whole new quality of community life possible: no self-conceit, no provoking, no envy (5:26).

How can we demonstrate this new reality? How can we break out of our religion, our ritual and our morality? Bruce Larson has recently said, "Christ did not come to bring goodness, but newness." For Paul we must modify this: Christ came to give us goodness before the Father which evidences itself in newness before men. But goodness must lead to newness and in this Bruce is correct. The test is serving love. By that test have we been born again?

6. Personal—When I was fifteen years of age I entered into life in the Spirit, but my walking in the Spirit has been inconsistent, to say the least.

As a new Christian I began to compare myself with my older brothers and sisters. I wanted to be like them to insure their acceptance and worked hard to accomplish it. This led to looking down on other struggling Christians who were not as serious or rigorous as I was.

Again and again, temptation would overwhelm me. There was the problem of lust which meant that my sexual desires could not be fulfilled overtly. This often shoved them into my dreams and fantasies. Then there was the problem of my intellectual pride. Since I was not athletic,

I achieved in books. Bible study came easily to me. I judged those for whom it was difficult as unspiritual.

Then, when I entered into the ministry, there was the problem of religious performance. I learned how to speak well, pray eloquently, and achieve in the church. Those who were not as able as I were held to be unfit and probably uncalled.

Paul's word judges all of this. "If we live by the Spirit, let us also walk by the Spirit." Since God has done it all in authoring my Christian life, I must let him do it all in sustaining that life. Continual dependence upon him will liberate me from my pretension as a Christian.

Questions for Discussion and Reflection: Chapter 5

5:1

1. What am I free from? Illustrate.
2. What am I free for? Illustrate.
3. How has God helped me to learn the true meaning of freedom?

5:2–12

4. What in our Christian communication flatters our egos? What convicts them?
5. How do I react to Paul's strong warning of falling from grace?
6. Why is law such a personal threat to my relationship with Christ?
7. Why am I so often guilty of playing at morality?

5:13–15

8. How is my faith demonstrated? Illustrate.
9. What is the content of my Christian love? Explain.
10. How does love fulfill the law for me?
11. Whose feet can I wash today?

5:16–24

12. "So you are a Christian? Welcome to the warfare." How do I react to that statement?
13. When I read over the works of the flesh, what does God say to me about my life?
14. When I read over the fruit of the Spirit, how can I see that translated into relationships around me? Be specific!

5:25–26

15. How can I take my walk in the Spirit today? Where will I place my feet?
16. How does goodness lead to newness in me?
17. How can I cultivate an attitude of continual dependence upon the Spirit?

6
Galatians
6:1-5

6 Brethren, if a man is overtaken in any trespass, you who are spiritual should restore him in a spirit of gentleness. Look to yourself, lest you too be tempted. ² Bear one another's burdens, and so fulfill the law of Christ. ³ For if any one thinks he is something, when he is nothing, he deceives himself. ⁴ But let each one test his own work, and then his reason to boast will be in himself alone and not in his neighbor. ⁵ For each man will have to bear his own load.

1. Language

STYLE—Paul continues his exhortation with explanation. "You should restore him" (6:1). "Look to yourself" (6:1). "Bear one another's burdens" (6:2). "But let each one test his own work" (6:4).

2. Historical—While the subject matter suggests that there are moral problems in Galatia and at least two groups, the fallen and the spiritual (6:1), it is questionable that Paul is writing to a specific need. He often concludes his letters with exhortation which applies to human nature in general and this is probably an example here. At least Paul assumes that some of the Galatians, "you who are spiritual," have remained strong in the faith. But if this were not the case he probably would have not written this letter.

3. Theological—As noted in 5:16 ff. Paul does not teach perfectionism. While those who engage in a life-style of the "works of the flesh" (5:19 ff.) cannot inherit the kingdom, Christians can and do sin (6:1).

Even the "spiritual" who are to restore them must struggle against temptation, thus the warfare of flesh and Spirit is theirs to fight too (6:1).

Since Paul has talked about specific sins and warned about gratifying the desires of the flesh, the question comes—what of those who have failed? Are they lost? No, says Paul, they are to be restored. But those who are involved in the process are to guard themselves too. The sin into which others fall has an attraction to us. And if not, then we are in danger of pride, which is also sin. If the Devil cannot get us one way, he will get us another.

The Christian who cares for others fulfills the "law of Christ" which is the law of love (5:14). Again Paul warns of arrogance in this ministry: "For if anyone thinks he is something, when he is nothing, he deceives himself" (6:3). A major part of our pastoral concern comes from empathy which flows from our own weakness and struggle.

On the road to maturity, however, we must grow to accept responsibility for ourselves. Dependence upon the brethren must become independence, where we simply stand before Christ. Thus, we are to test ourselves. "But let each one test his own work" (6:4). We are to examine our own moral character, being honest about our sin, and just as honest about Christ's forgiveness. Finally, the man in Christ will "boast . . . in himself alone and not in his neighbor" (6:4). He will be accountable to Christ and free from neurotic dependence upon a Christian environment to support his faith and life. Paul concludes, "For each man will have to bear his own load" (6:5). I take this to be at the Day of Judgment.

The movement then is from bearing each other's burdens (6:2) to bearing our own load (6:5). While we will all be tempted, those who are *spiritual*, walking by the Spirit, are to restore those who yield to the temptation. This interdependence (6:2) must have as its goal self-testing where each person stands before Christ, for on the Day of Judgment we cannot blame each other. Then we are simply accountable to Christ for what we have done with our Christian freedom.

4. Strategic—Paul recalls the Galatians to their personal responsibility in caring for each other. Rather than rejecting any brother, they are to restore him. The schism in Galatia will be healed by the burden-bearing community. Paul's intention is not only to castigate his opponents, but also to heal wounds, to rebuke those who may have fallen into sin and to build a positive, healthy body of believers. Thus, beyond the polemic in this letter is its pastoral concern. Paul defends his authority

and message to summon the Galatians back to their simple faith that they may grow up into maturity. Here, in this exhortation, we uncover the deeper concern of the Apostle. He writes, not merely to justify himself, or to instruct the churches in the truth of the faith, but also to move them on the road to growth in Christ, and to prepare them for the Day of Judgment. Because Paul believes that is where we are going, and that our final test will be alone before God (6:5), he expends himself that we may be ready for that day.

5. Contemporary—Since the world assumes that the church is a place for good people, and since we share that assumption, there is no discipline among Christians today. If one falls into a trespass he is overlooked, judged or perhaps pitied, but not restored. If he is confronted by his failure, it is not in a "spirit of gentleness" (6:1), coming out of the admission of our own weakness and temptation, but in a spirit of adversity.

What a revolution if we really believed and experienced the church as a place for the weak and broken of this world. What if we were free to share our real temptations and failures? What if people loved us enough not to let us continue on our destructive course, but to call us on our sin? What if we really did bear each other's burdens, shattering the shell of our loneliness? Would not the world pound down our door for that kind of life?

Burden bearing requires burden sharing. If I do not share my burden, then I refuse to let my brother fulfill the law of Christ (6:2). What pride to say, "No one would understand my problem. No one would really care about me." As we share with those who are spiritual, they will gladly bear with us, and a crucial part of God's method for maturity will become ours. A lonely Christian is a defeated Christian. God means for us to bear each other in order that we may stand alone. If we deny the process we frustrate the result, our maturity in Christ, and the world sees the hollow shell of our "goodness" masking the lonely burdens which slowly crush us.

6. Personal—It has been only recently that I have been able to exercise some moral discipline among my converts. For a long time I was too insecure to do this. I feared rejection and I assumed that my own moral struggles disqualified me, not realizing that honesty about my struggle gave the "spirit of gentleness" I needed for the ministry of restoration.

I have come to see, however, that if I really love people with Christ's love and not simply with my own neurotic and possessive love, then for his sake and theirs I must risk rejection.

We were planning a trip to Wichita, Kansas, involving twenty-five people. The civic center was rented for five days of concerts and evangelistic preaching. One of my dearest friends and brothers and one of the most talented musicians among us was to be part of our team. His life, however, was in troubled times. Part of the problem was the very ability he had as a musician which turned the stage into an ego-trip. I knew that if he went with us he would be a fantastic communicator, yet he would compromise our witness. So we had it out, and I told him he could not go. He was living with me at the time and this precipitated his leaving our house. I said good-bye in the driveway as he loaded his things into his car. We were both crying. He drove away and I felt empty and shaken. During our five days of meetings in Wichita over 400 people received Christ and major parts of the city were touched with the gospel. My friend? He joined us not to perform but to simply be part of our fellowship. We had taken a step toward maturity and God honored us for it. These verses must be operative in the church for any spiritual health.

Galatians
6:6

6 Let him who is taught the word share all good things with him who teaches.

1. Language

STYLE—exhortation, "Let him . . ."

2. Historical—No added information.

3. Theological—Paul exhorts here in the inter-responsibility of those teaching and taught. This parallels our moral inter-responsibility in 6:2. Some have taken the "share all good things" to be Paul's polite way of saying "pay your teachers." Paul, however, is not shy to say this directly when needed.

It is better to see this as the mutual growth process between the teacher and his students. As we are taught the word we should respond in sharing our insights with our teacher. Thus we learn together as we grow into Christ.

4. Strategic—Nothing appears added here.

5. Contemporary—Once again we learn that Christians need each other to grow. Communication is two-way. Sermons and lectures can keep us from each other, especially if we are barricaded behind the authority of the pulpit. We must have two-way teaching situations in the church for real growth to go on.

6. Personal—I have been teaching Paul's letters at Claremont's Men's College. My students turned in their answers to inductive questions, and from them I had a continual flow of insight and information. Not only did I learn new things from their study of the text, but I also learned about the students whom I was teaching. The adage, "we teach pupils, not subjects," is, at least in part, true. This feedback guided me in my lectures and assignments. I was able to spot their needs and weaknesses and address myself to the real issues of their lives. True teaching is an intensely personal matter, not only mind to mind but heart to heart. The "sharing of all good things" makes this possible.

Galatians
6:7–10

7 Do not be deceived; God is not mocked, for whatever a man sows, that he will also reap. ⁸ For he who sows to his own flesh will from the flesh reap corruption; but he who sows to the Spirit will from the Spirit reap eternal life. ⁹ And let us not grow weary in well-doing, for in due season we shall reap, if we do not lose heart. ¹⁰ So then, as we have opportunity, let us do good to all men, and especially to those who are of the household of faith.

1. Language

STYLE—The exhortation with explanation continues: "Do not be deceived" (6:7). "And let us not . . ." (6:9). "So then, as we have opportunity let us" (6:10). Note the agricultural image at the core of the passage.

2. **Historical**—No new information about Paul, the Galatians, or their opponents is offered.

3. **Theological**—Paul drives to his conclusion. He shows by introducing the flesh and the Spirit again that this has dominated his thought since 5:13. The actualization of our freedom in loving service is done through the power of the Spirit. This, however, does not suspend our moral responsibility. We are growing the field of our life, we must choose how we do it.

God has established the principle of sowing and reaping as a fundamental law of all nature. This cannot be violated. We cannot fill our minds with evil and lust and then pray for God to deliver us by a miracle. The law of sowing and reaping operates. What we place in our minds will come out in our attitudes and actions. We cannot act in an unchristian way with people and still praise God. What we do will determine who we are.

We choose each day to either sow to the flesh or the Spirit. When we study the Word of God, read helpful Christian books, pray and share our faith, have fellowship with other Christians, and especially meet the needs of our neighbors, we sow to the Spirit. We are creatures, in part, of our environment and our conscious acts, and the reinforcement we receive from others determines much of the direction of our life.

Paul promises that this spiritual sowing will end in eternal life. The question is not how far along I am on the way, but the direction in which I am moving. The Apostle knows that this sowing is for a lifetime. Thus he warns us about growing "weary in well-doing" (6:9). We are in it for the long haul. But the goal is certain—reaping the reward of our sowing which will in the end be eternity with Christ (6:8). Along the way God will show us enough fruit to encourage us, but not too much to make us complacent.

While our sowing to the Spirit is, in part, the development of our inner spiritual life, Paul throws his weight on doing "good to all men," especially fellow Christians, "the household of faith" (6:10). Thus, once again, we see that the growth of our spiritual life is dependent upon the quality of our relationships, not just our quiet time. As we do good to all men, we sow to the Spirit and build for eternity.

4. Strategic—Paul has warned of returning to bondage. He has shown how the law reveals and restrains sin but cannot change the inner man. The flesh can be sown not only by sinful acts, but also by rigorous morality when it is based on human effort to gratify our own egos. All of this will lead to corruption (6:8).

New life in the Spirit, however, does not absolve us from good works, as the legalists suppose. We are to "do good to all men," not in order to be righteous, but because we have been accepted as righteous in Christ and received his Spirit.

Thus, paradoxically, the free man in Christ will display good works in the world. But he does it, not for his salvation, but *from* his salvation. With faith's assurance, in joyous abandon, we reach out to all with the love of Christ.

5. Contemporary—Our culture denies the law of sowing and reaping. We assume that we can sow sex and violence on television and in motion pictures and not reap anarchy. We assume that we can sow secularism in the classroom and not reap irreligion. We assume we can sow materialism as the goal for business and not reap political corruption and empty lives. The Devil has fooled us again.

Because the law of sowing and reaping cannot be violated, we must look to ourselves, our families and our culture. We must be involved in the political process. We must care about what floods the media. We must examine the textbooks. If our nation continues to sow to the flesh, the end can only be corruption. God will not be mocked.

6. Personal—How do I relate to the law of sowing and reaping? What shapes my assumptions, values and goals? What books and articles do I read? What do I dwell on in my spare moments? What disciplines and commitments have I made for a growing spiritual life?

What of my relationships? Do I reach out in love to those about me? Am I vulnerable to them? Do I respond to need when I see it?

All of these are hard questions and deserve careful, thoughtful answers. I have long struggled for some kind of ordered devotional life, and most of the time I have been unsuccessful. One helpful conclusion I have reached is to discover where there is structure and order in my day and then tag on spiritual activity at that point.

For example, my wife and I had a difficult time reading and praying together in the first year of our marriage. In looking over our life, I discovered that we were together most of the time for breakfast. This meant that we could share devotions together at the table if we worked at it. A devotional book now resides in the dining room and it is natural for us to read and pray together as we begin our day. Build on your good habits and they will become more and more natural.

Galatians
6:11–16

11 See with what large letters I am writing to you with my own hand. [12] It is those who want to make a good showing in the flesh that would compel you to be circumcised, and only in order that they may not be persecuted for the cross of Christ. [13] For even those who receive circumcision do not themselves keep the law, but they desire to have you circumcised that they may glory in your flesh. [14] But far be it from me to glory except in the cross of our Lord Jesus Christ, by which the world has been crucified to me, and I to the world. [15] For neither circumcision counts for anything, nor uncircumcision, but a new creation. [16] Peace and mercy be upon all who walk by this rule, upon the Israel of God.

1. Language

VOCABULARY—*A new creation:* conversion. *The Israel of God:* all true sons of Abraham by faith, Jew and Gentile.

STYLE—Paul has ended his exhortation. He now picks up the pen himself. "See with what large letters I am writing to you with my own hand" (6:11). This is his way of autographing his letter. He takes a parting shot at the legalists and gives a final witness himself. A blessing appears in 6:16.

2. Historical

—Paul writes the final conclusion himself (6:11). He will glory not in the flesh, but in the cross where he has died to this world's opinions about him (6:14).

The legalists, motivated by ego, want to "make a good showing in the flesh" (6:12) by compelling the Galatians to be circumcised. In this they avoid the offense of the cross, that is, that we can do nothing for our salvation (6:12, see 5:11). In making a good showing in the flesh and glorifying in the flesh (6:13) Paul has a play on words. The mark of circumcision, it is supposed, makes the flesh look good to God, but it is a fleshly act and only makes a person look good to those living a worldly life.

The legalists, furthermore, "do not themselves keep the law." They only select parts of it that please them. This exposes their insincerity.

3. **Theological**—Paul renounces the legalists because they are:
1. Determined by worldly values.
2. Avoiding the offense of the cross.
3. Selective in their interpretation of the law.
In other words, they are hypocrites.

In contrast, the Apostle has renounced selfish values, dying to the world (6:14). Rather than avoiding the offense of the cross, he glories in it (6:14). He has transcended the old divisions; circumcision and uncircumcision, finding a new creation in Christ (6:15).

All who walk by the rule, not of the law, but of the new creation, receive peace and mercy (6:16). They are the true Israel of God, the Israel after the Spirit, the sons of Abraham by faith.

Thus, Paul ends where he begins (3:1), at the cross. But here the cross is applied personally not just theologically. Because he is a free man in Christ, he is relieved from public opinion and performance. He determines to glory in the cross, to live at the cross. This is the sign of the end: the end of the law, of sin and of judgment. This is the sign of life: forgiveness and freedom. Here evangelical Christianity will take its stand: "far be it from me to glory except in the cross of our Lord Jesus Christ" (6:14).

4. **Strategic**—Paul rebukes the methods (circumcision) and motives (pride) of the legalists. His accusation is pointed, "even those who receive circumcision do not themselves keep the law" (6:13). He writes as a strict Jew, who fully kept the law and then abandoned all for Christ (1:11–17).

The sham of the legalists appears in their unwillingness to embrace the totality of the law. This insincerity denies them any respect from Paul and exposes their evil motives. Paul is saying, "If you really want the Old Covenant, don't become a legalistic Christian, go all the way, become a Pharisee, a true Jew. Don't just play with the law. Its demands are too great. For the sake of integrity, it is all or nothing."

The true Israel, however, is not the legalists, but those who share the new creation. They receive God's power and mercy (6:16).

5. Contemporary—In the church today we play with the law and reveal our insincerity. We award gold stars for memory verses and laud those who tithe and act properly, but we tend to avoid the real questions: How do you treat your wife? How is your integrity in business? Do you spend time with your kids? Are you open about your faith? This double standard blurs the sharpness of our witness.

At the same time, we wink at the world's hypocrisy. We fail to demand honesty in government. We "understand" why corporations feel obliged to make illegal campaign gifts to political parties. We shrug off violence on the screen and on the streets. Pornography is someone else's problem. Drugs are illegal, but alcoholism is accepted. Racism is "bad" but our neighborhood remains closed. We plead "property values" to maintain our social isolation.

To church and world, Paul replies that all that counts is a "new creation" (6:15). If God does not re-create from within we will only continue the double standard and wonder why our children renounce us. To transcend the old polarities, "neither circumcision counts for anything, nor uncircumcision" (6:15), God must act, and he has. A whole new beginning opens up for us in Christ.

6. Personal—It is the demonstration of the new creation which I must be about. How easy it has been for me to seek the comfort of my own kind, even my Christian kind. Do I prefer Presbyterians to Pentecostals? Do I demand liturgy rather that "holy hilarity"? I am still caught in the either/or of circumcision or uncircumcision, while God wants me to discover a new creation. A grey-haired saint stops me and I discover the radiance of Christ—a new creation. Some black men come from Harlem and I find them brothers, a new creation. A drug addict meets Christ and roots himself in my heart—a new creation. Here is the validity of my faith.

I will never forget a call from a lawyer friend in Houston. Could I visit his mother and father in Whittier? Both in their eighties, they had just become Christians, and his mother was dying of cancer.

I walked into the motel wondering what I would find. Here was a frail woman propped into a chair. Her husband, eyes enlarged through thick glasses, welcomed me with a hearty handshake.

I sat on the edge of the bed as they told me of their time in the northwest and a small church in which they had been "saved." Now they had begun to read the Bible and pray together. They asked me if what they had believed in the church was true to the Bible and I assured them that it was.

The little wife told me how thankful she was for her cancer because it had brought her to Christ as she had gone to the church seeking healing. She rejoiced that all her sins over the years were now cancelled and forgiven.

Her husband told me that he had lived an independent and successful life. Now, at eighty-four, he was having to trust Christ for the future and it was a new adventure. After prayer I left the motel humbled and grateful. Here were two new Christians, their lives behind them, acting like teenagers home from a summer conference. There was a light in their eyes and a freshness in their exhausted bodies. This is all that counts, a new creation. May God burn that truth into my heart.

Galatians
6:17

17 Henceforth let no man trouble me; for I bear
on my body the marks of Jesus.

1. Language

STYLE—a final affirmation and witness.

2. Historical—Paul bears the marks of Jesus. This probably means his scars from beatings and persecution (see 2 Cor. 11:23–29). Thus his body bears witness to the offense of the gospel and his faithfulness to Christ.

3. Theological—Paul's witness is in word, deed and suffering. It is in suffering that we learn who we really are as our defenses are shedded. The Apostle re-values pain under the shadow of the cross. We instinctively run from danger ("self-preservation"). While Paul does not seek it, he takes it and the stripes and scars are his badges of faithfulness to Christ. Nietzsche talked of "bloody truths," which men would die for. Paul held such truths. You could beat him, but not crush him, and his scars were welcomed as "marks of Jesus." Because God brought the miracle of redemption from Christ's agony, we can trust him to teach us and use us through our suffering in this world. Some Christians hope for Jesus to come and deliver us from tribulation. But I think not.

Christ will not deliver us from that which he uses for our refinement and his glory. The world must wonder at the "bloody Christians" with their "bloody truths" in Caesar's arenas.

4. Strategic—Paul, by his final affirmation, expresses his freedom. No man can trouble him, he is tried and tested. His body is his witness. Such is the one who the legalists are unable to confound in Galatia.

5. Contemporary—Where are our "bloody Christians" with their "bloody truths"? The world watches. Where will we draw the line? Where will we confess our faith? Where will we shed our blood? It is the "bloody truths" that have sent people into the streets, and we have them. Life is only worth living when I have something to die for—better, when I have someone to die for.

6. Personal—I have been asked, "Don, if someone put a machine gun in your gut and asked you to renounce Christ or die, would you do it?" I have to answer in honesty, I do not know. But I pray God that in that hour I would receive the grace to stand for him.

If this body must go to the grave, may it bear, O God, the marks of Jesus.

Galatians
6:18

18 The grace of our Lord Jesus Christ be with your spirit, brethren. Amen.

1. Language

VOCABULARY—*Amen:* truly, for sure.

STYLE—Liturgical, benediction.

2. Historical—Nothing appears new about Paul, the Galatians, or their opponents.

3. Theological—Only by the "grace of our Lord Jesus Christ . . . with your spirit" will the gospel prosper again in Galatia.

Although Paul could not open the letter with a prayer of thanksgiving, he can conclude with a benediction. Even though the Galatians have faltered, God remains faithful.

4. Strategic—In the final benediction, Paul calls the Galatians "brethren" and draws them back to himself. He loves them, because they are "brethren." Paul expresses confidence, not in the legalists, or even in himself, and certainly not in the Galatians, but in the "grace of our Lord Jesus Christ."

5. Contemporary—What is the last word in this world? Is it death, catastrophe, the fall of another empire? It is not. The last word is the grace of our Lord Jesus Christ. So we must hold out our hands to bless, when all else curse. Since we come with the blessing—the grace of Christ—we are God's sign in this world that there is another destiny beyond the battle. When the *Amen* is said there is nothing else to be said. Grace is final and sufficient.

6. Personal—What is the blessing of my life to others? Is it grace? What is the last word they hear from me? Is it *grace?*

I am always interested in the final words of a dying man. What sums up his life, I wonder? Well, what is my last word? What do people think of when they remember me? The grace of Christ, or a good guy? The grace of Christ, or a fine person, a laugh, a life of the party?

Joe Blinco was an associate evangelist for the Billy Graham team. He came from an alcoholic's home in the slums of England and was converted as a young man. Joe feared no one. When he died, I summed up Joe to the gathering. "When you met Joe Blinco, in ten minutes you learned two things. Number one, Joe loved you. Number two, Joe loved Christ." The "grace of our Lord Jesus Christ be with your spirit. Amen." May it be so through you and through me.

Questions for Discussion and Reflection: Chapter 6

6:1–5

1. How have I dealt with a fallen brother or sister?
2. What is the attitude of my fellow Christians toward those who are caught in some sin?
3. How honest am I about my own temptations? How do I deal with them? What attitude would this give me toward the sins of others?

4. How serious am I about the Day of Judgment? Am I preparing for that Day? What is my attitude as I think about it?

6:6

5. Who am I teaching? Who am I sharing with? How much of my communication is really two-way?

6:7–10

6. What am I sowing? What am I reaping?
7. How can I sow to the Spirit? How has my life demonstrated the law of sowing and reaping?
8. Do I view my Christian life as a sprint or a long distance race?

6:11–16

9. What does it mean to me to glory in the cross?
10. What does it mean to live at the cross in my church, my family, my business, my relationships?
11. How is the new creation demonstrated in me?

6:17

12. Where are my "marks of Jesus?" How is suffering a part of my Christian life-style?

6:18

13. How is my life a sign of God's blessing in this world? Where are the other signs around me? Can I identify them today?